THE
SPURS
MISCELLANY

To Cath, Daniel and Tom – the best home team in the world

To Jo, Ellen, Carla, and Ruby, Mum, Maxine, Nicola and Simone

THE
SPURS
MISCELLANY

BY ADAM POWLEY
AND MARTIN CLOAKE

VSP

Vision Sports Publishing
2 Coombe Gardens,
London, SW20 0QU

www.visionsp.co.uk

Published by
Vision Sports Publishing in 2007

ISBN 10: 1-905326-32-7
ISBN 13: 978-1-905326-32-7

Printed and bound in the UK by
Cromwell Press, Trowbridge, Wilts

Typeset by Palimpsest Book Production Limited,
Grangemouth, Stirlingshire

A CIP catalogue record for this book is
available from the British Library

Foreword

By Steve Perryman

In 125 years of football, Tottenham Hotspur has crammed in more history than most clubs. This great little book gives a real flavour of what the club has achieved and what it means to the people who are, or ever have been, associated with it.

When the club celebrated its 100th year in 1982 I had the privilege of leading a side that was full of confidence, confidence that came off the back of our win at Wembley in that wonderful FA Cup final against Manchester City. The confidence came from a belief in playing attacking football, the Tottenham way, and it stood us in good stead when we played Chelsea at Stamford Bridge in the quarter final. We'd got off to a slow start and Chelsea took the lead, before we stepped up a gear and scored three in ten minutes. I think we only really played like a Spurs team should for those 10 minutes in that game, but it was enough to see us through - and we went on to retain the Cup.

I reckon there's a very good chance the current team can do what we did, and celebrate an important date in the club's history by lifting some silverware. Once they do that, anything is possible, because once you've been a winner you want the taste again and again.

I know I'll always be associated with the club in people's minds, hardly surprising after playing over 1,000 games in the famous shirt, but the funny thing is that Spurs didn't mean that much to me before I signed for them. In fact, I'd never seen them play before they asked me to sign – I was a west London boy and I used to go to Brentford and QPR with my brothers. But my love affair with Spurs started when I walked through the doors of the club.

There was a feeling of warmth and belonging there. I felt it was a place where you'd get an even break, where you'd be rewarded if you worked hard and with honesty. I still firmly believe that the key to the game is about how players fit with a club, and I felt I fitted with the ethics of Tottenham Hotspur. Much of that was to do with Bill Nicholson, the best football man I ever had the pleasure of working with.

Quite rightly, Bill features large in this book, as do the club's supporters, who Bill always said were the most important people. "They will be here when we're gone," he'd say. "And the most important are the season ticket holders, because they put their money up front before they've even seen a ball kicked. They are paying for hope, and that's what we've got to give them."

There's plenty to read here about Tottenham's fans, some great anecdotes, some wonderful stuff about the derbies with Arsenal – they really did matter to us as much as they did to the fans – and some facts which demonstrate the strength and loyalty of a wonderful set of supporters. I really do believe the fans played their part when they followed us in such numbers through Division Two after we were relegated in 1977. That was one of the most enjoyable seasons I had, and it shows again how important that fit is – the fans demanded our commitment by showing theirs, and that's the key to the Tottenham crowd.

No true Tottenham fan can fail to be fascinated by this cracking little book. From records of the club's proud history, to tales of classic matches – like the 1981 FA Cup semi at Highbury, wonderful! – and even how many pies were eaten at the 1901 FA Cup Final, there's plenty for everyone. There's also plenty of stuff on the lighter side of the game to keep you amused, and I seem to feature quite a few times here too.

Come On You Spurs.

Steve Perryman

Thanks

Our thanks go first and foremost to Jim Drewett, whose vision, advice, support and faith have been invaluable.

Jim Duggan's keen eye for detail has proved vital, as has his outstanding knowledge and appreciation of the culture of supporting Tottenham Hotspur. The *From The Lane* messageboard has been a constant source of stimulation (thanks in particular to Lyndon Brown and Winky), as have the various matchday crews down the years. Bernie Kingsley, Tony Fuller, and Joel Miller have also provided valuable assistance.

Nigel Waters has taken much time out of a busy schedule to respond to our questions, and has provided some valuable contacts. Thanks also to Keith Burkinshaw and John Syer for their time and trust.

Special thanks to Steve Perryman. Still the captain.

Many thanks to Bob Bond for his excellent illustrations.

Thanks also to Toby Trotman at VSP, Janice Jaggers, Cheryl Foreman, Julie Bracey, Karen Buchanan, Keith Kendrick for his understanding, Andrew Shields, Pete Panayi, St Bonaventure school, The Latymer School Edmonton, Neal Cobourne, Steve Davis, Troy Hagan, Paolo Hewitt, Danny Keene, Andy Porter and Bob Goodwin and to Clive Batty for his advice, plus the seasoned pros of FC Lumbago.

Last but not least thank you to all the players, officials and supporters of the world famous Tottenham Hotspur Football Club.

Authors' note: All stats in the Spurs Miscellany are correct up until the start of the 2007/08 season.

— IN THE BEGINNING —

Hotspur Football Club was formed on Tuesday September 5th 1882 by a group of schoolboys who had played cricket under the name of the Hotspur Cricket Club. The cricket club had been formed two years earlier by pupils of St John's Middle Class School and some friends at Tottenham Grammar School.

With the end of the cricket season in September, the boys wanted another sporting pursuit to fill the winter months, and decided to form an association football club. The decision was taken at a street meeting beneath a lamp-post on the corner of Tottenham High Road and Park Lane.

The 11 founder members, all schoolboys, were: E Beaven, Bobby Buckle (captain), Fred Dexter, Stuart Lehman (goalkeeper), E Wall, and three sets of brothers, J and T Anderson, Lindsay and Hamilton (commonly known as Ham or Sam) Casey, and Jack and Peter Thompson.

— DOUBLE DOIN' RECORD BREAKIN' HOTSPURS —

Tottenham Hotspur were the first club side in the modern game to win the League and FA Cup Double, in 1960/61 – the feat had previously only been achieved by Preston in 1888/89 and Aston Villa in 1896/97. In the course of achieving this record success, the team played thrilling football and set a host of other records:

Most wins in First Division history (31)

Most away wins in First Division history (16)

Champions with fewest players used (17)

Most consecutive wins at the start of a season (11) – still a top-flight record

Fastest achievement of 50 points (29 games)

Scored most league goals in club history (115); runners-up Sheffield Wednesday mustered only 78 by comparison

Equalled Arsenal's record of 33 away points in a single campaign

Beat 11 clubs twice to equal the record number of 'doubles' set by Manchester United (1956/57) and Wolves (1958/59)

Equalled record number of points won in a season in which two points counted for a win (66), which had been set by Arsenal in 1930/31

— INTERNATIONAL BRIGHT YOUNG THING —

When Aaron Lennon came on as a 58th minute substitute in England's World Cup match against Trinidad & Tobago on June 15th 2006, he became the youngest Spurs player ever to play in the World Cup Finals. He was just 19 years and 60 days old, three years younger than previous record holder Jimmy Greaves, who was 22 years and 100 days old when he took the field for England's game against Hungary on June 8th 1958 in Sweden.

Lennon is also the youngest ever Spur to win full international honours. He takes the record from the legendary Jimmy Dimmock, who was 20 years and 125 days old when he turned out for England against Scotland on April 9th 1921.

— WHAT'S IN THE NAME? —

It's one of the most famous and distinctive names in sport. Not for Spurs the prosaic 'city', 'united', or even the more poetic 'albion' sported by other clubs. The young lads who formed the Hotspur cricket and then football club harked back to the days of medieval chivalry and derring-do for inspiration in choosing their name.

The 'Hotspur' in Tottenham's name refers to the nickname of Henry Percy (1366–1403), a descendant of one of the most famous and powerful noble families of the Middle Ages. The Percys had arrived with William the Conqueror from Normandy and were tasked with subduing the rebellious north and keeping marauding Scots in check. For this they were handsomely rewarded and effectively became monarchs of the region.

Their power base was in Northumberland and the family seat was Alnwick Castle, the stand-in for Hogwarts School in the *Harry Potter* films. Henry Percy had a reputation for being a bit of a troublemaker and rogue. To put it bluntly, young Henry liked a punch-up. He took part in his first battle at the age of eight and was knighted at 11; a statue of him sited in Northumberland Avenue in Newcastle portrays him drawing his sword as if ready for an imminent confrontation.

Percy got his nickname 'Harry Hotspur', owing to his particularly enthusiastic use of riding spurs when charging into battle. It also refers to his hot-headed nature and a tendency to act first, think later. He was immortalised by William Shakespeare in *Henry IV*, and makes a typically dramatic entrance in Act 5, scene IV:

HOTSPUR: My name is Harry Percy.
PRINCE HENRY: Why, then I see a very valiant rebel of the name.

(. . . **they fight**)

Arguments over money to fund the real Harry Hotspur's various battles and the King's refusal to let him ransom captured Scottish nobles inevitably led to further confrontation, and matters came to a decisive head at the Battle of Shrewsbury between the crown and rebellious lords in 1403. With a typical mix of daring and recklessness, Hotspur charged King Henry's line. After he was thrown off his horse and killed in hand-to-hand combat, his body was beheaded, quartered and taken on a tour around the country.

With his swashbuckling reputation romanticised over the years, hundreds of years later the boys who formed Spurs found inspiration in his name when deciding upon one for their club. And with its credentials reinforced by the local links – the Percy clan had extensive land interests in what is now the Tottenham area and the club's first administrative base was the YMCA's Percy House in Northumberland Park – the fledgling football club was christened 'Hotspur' (becoming Tottenham Hotspur in 1885) and a football legend was born.

[Note: The name was also adopted by the famously swashbuckling comic for boys, *Hotspur*, which was published between 1933 and 1981].

Harry Hotspur

— BIG LEAGUE —

Formed in 1882, Tottenham Hotspur did not make their league debut until September 24th 1892, when they played an away game against Polytechnic in the Southern Alliance. Spurs won 2–1, thanks to goals from Sykes and Brigden, and went on to finish third, with a record that read:

P	W	D	L	F	A	Pts
12	7	2	3	29	21	16

Since then, Spurs have played in the Southern League, United League, Thames and Medway League, Southern District Combination, Western League, London Football Combination, World War 1 League, World War 2 League, London League, Football League South, Football League and Premier League.

The club's overall record in all league games* is:

P	W	D	L	F	A	Pts
4,547	1,968	1,079	1,500	7,699	6,306	5,433

*Correct up to start of 2007/08 season.

— FA CUP KINGS —

Tottenham's reputation as a cup team rests largely on the club's record in the FA Cup. Spurs have won the trophy eight times, with only Arsenal (9) and Manchester United (11) winning on more occasions. In 1901 they were the first, and remain the only, non-league team to win the FA Cup, beating Sheffield United.

What's more, the Lilywhites have only lost one of the nine FA Cup finals they have played in, going down 3–2 to Coventry City in 1987. The club's winning FA Cup Final appearances are:

Date	Venue	Result	Scorers
1901	Crystal Palace	Tottenham 2 Sheffield United 2	Brown 2
1901 (Replay)	Burnden Park	Tottenham 3 Sheffield United 1	Cameron, Smith T, Brown
1921	Stamford Bridge	Tottenham 1 Wolves 0	Dimmock
1961	Wembley	Tottenham 2 Leicester City 0	Smith R, Dyson

1962	Wembley	Tottenham 3	Blanchflower
		Burnley 1	(p), Smith R,
			Greaves
1967	Wembley	Tottenham 2	Robertson,
		Chelsea 1	Saul
1981	Wembley	Tottenham 1	
		Manchester City 1	Hutchinson og
1981	Wembley	Tottenham 3	Villa 2, Crooks
(Replay)		Manchester City 2	
1982	Wembley	Tottenham 1	Hoddle
		QPR 1	
1982	Wembley	Tottenham 1	Hoddle (p)
(Replay)		QPR 0	
1991	Wembley	Tottenham 2	Stewart,
		Nottingham Forest 1	Walker og

Over the years, Spurs have played a total of 391 FA Cup games, winning 203, drawing a further 97 and losing 91. In doing so they have scored 776 goals and conceded 466. The biggest win came on February 3rd 1960 when a fourth-round replay against Crewe Alexandra at White Hart Lane saw Spurs run out 13–2 winners.

— THE SEEDS OF A GREAT RIVALRY —

The fierce rivalry between Tottenham and Arsenal dates back to the early years of the 20th century. It was sparked by the manner in which the Gunners arrived in north London, and fuelled by the controversial decision to award Arsenal a place in the top-flight – at Tottenham's expense.

By 1908 the club which started life as Dial Square – and which became first Royal Arsenal, then Woolwich Arsenal, then The Arsenal before settling on simply Arsenal – had already become Tottenham's biggest rivals as the only London team in the First Division. But in 1913 the south Londoners were transplanted into their rivals' front yard.

The controversial move was the brainchild of an ambitious estate agent and Tory councillor called Henry Norris. He was a director at Fulham and had been trying to merge the west Londoners with Arsenal. But when the League ruled the new club would have to play in the Second Division, Norris decided Woolwich Arsenal had greater potential on their own – but only if they could be moved from Plumstead to somewhere with better transport links and a catchment area with greater potential support.

So in 1910/11, with Arsenal on the verge of bankruptcy, Norris stepped in to buy the club, and began to build for the future. He identified a suitable site in North London, the sports ground of St John's College of Divinity. It had excellent transport links and was in the middle of a residential area. But it was also in Highbury, literally just down the road from Tottenham.

Spurs and Clapton Orient objected to the move, as did local residents, but the League was powerless to prevent it and Highbury opened for business in September 1913.

By now, however, Arsenal were in the Second Division, while Spurs remained in the top flight. But the storm clouds were gathering over Europe and in 1915 the Football League was suspended as World War I raged on mainland Europe, with Spurs and Chelsea bottom of the First Division table. Arsenal were sixth in Division Two.

When competition finally resumed in 1919, the League decided to increase the number of First Division clubs by two to 22. Precedent suggested Spurs and Chelsea would not be relegated, while Derby County and Preston North End, the top two in the Second Division, would be promoted.

But Norris had been lobbying hard behind the scenes. He had invested a huge amount of money and needed to realise a return. He argued that, as Arsenal had been members of the league longer than Spurs, his club should be awarded Tottenham's place. Based on this logic both Wolverhampton Wanderers and Birmingham City, who finished in the places above Arsenal, had better claims.

The League met in March 1919. When the top division had been expanded in the past, all competing clubs had been put into a ballot, and the four with the most votes were adjudged to be the winners. But Liverpool chairman and League President John McKenna suggested that this time it should be different. He proposed Chelsea, who had finished a place above Spurs, should be automatically re-elected because their league position was a result of Liverpool losing to Manchester United in a game later found to have been fixed by a betting syndicate. The League agreed. McKenna then suggested that Derby County and Preston North End, who had topped Division Two, should also be promoted without a vote. Again, the meeting agreed.

That left Arsenal, Barnsley, Birmingham, Hull City and Wolves competing with Spurs for just one place, and each member club with just one vote to cast instead of their usual four. McKenna made an impassioned speech in favour of Arsenal. The Spurs contingent were shocked, and when the votes were counted Arsenal had 18 and Spurs eight. There was no logical reason for the decision, but Spurs had little choice but to accept it. Arsenal have since gone on to maintain their top-flight status, a record achievement coloured by the fact that they are the only team in the top division not to be promoted on playing merit.

— PARROT KILLERS —

After Spurs made a pioneering tour of Argentina and Uruguay in 1908, losing only one of the seven games played, they embarked on the long boat journey back home. During the trip, the squad entered a fancy dress competition, which was won by two members dressed as Robinson Crusoe and Man Friday. The costumes were rounded off by the ship's pet parrot, which was presented to the club by the ship's captain.

The bird was brought back to White Hart Lane where it perched happily for 11 years until it keeled over and died on the very day Arsenal were given Tottenham's place in the First Division in March 1919.

It's believed this is where perhaps the greatest football cliché of all, 'sick as parrot', originated.

— A COLOURFUL HISTORY —

Tottenham's colours have altered quite a bit since the early years, when the team turned out in a strip of navy blue. In 1885, three years after the club was formed, the kit changed to light blue and white halves in tribute to the Blackburn Rovers side that won the FA Cup that year for the second time in a row. Five years later, in a move that will amaze modern supporters, the kit changed again – this time to red shirts and navy shorts!

In 1896, a year after going professional and to celebrate the club's election to the Southern League, Tottenham adopted a kit described mouthwateringly as chocolate and gold stripes, colours then worn by Wolverhampton Wanderers. This tasty kit was worn until 1898, when the famous lilywhite shirts and navy shorts were first adopted as a mark of respect for Preston North End, who were the dominant team of the time.

From then on the team colours have remained virtually unchanged, although in the 1960s Spurs played in white shorts in Europe to create an all-white strip, a testimony to Bill Nicholson's admiration for the mighty Real Madrid (briefly also adopted for league matches in 1985 and for the 125th anniversary season 2007/08). The cockerel badge (See *Badge of Honour,* page 33) first appeared on the team's shirts in 1921.

The famous white shirt remained largely untouched for over a century until 2005 when the club accepted a design which featured navy sleeves.

— 'STEVIE, STEVIE, STEVIE, STEVIE PERRYMAN' —

Steve Perryman holds the record for the most appearances for Tottenham Hotspur. Between 1969 and 1986 he played for the first team 851 times, starting as a sub on only three occasions. This astonishing record is made up of 653 league games, 69 FA Cup matches, 66 League Cup appearances and 63 European ties. Defender/midfielder Steve scored 39 goals in all competitions.

Steve's record stands at 261 more than goalkeeper Pat Jennings, who made 590 appearances for Spurs between 1964 and 1977. Gary Mabbutt (585 games, 1982–98) and Cyril Knowles (504 games, 1964–75) are the other players who have turned out in the club's colours more than 500 times.

Steve Perryman after one of the more significant of his 851 games for Spurs

— EUROPEAN GLORY —

Spurs blazed a trail for British clubs in Europe, becoming the first British side to win a European trophy when they defeated Atletico Madrid 5–1 in the 1963 Cup Winners' Cup Final.

In Europe, up to the start of the 2007/08 season Spurs had played 109 matches, winning 67 (including one tie on penalties), drawing 20 and losing 22 in total in all three European competitions, scoring 238 and conceding 99 goals in the process. The biggest win in a European tie came on September 28th 1971 in the UEFA Cup, when Icelandic outfit Keflavik were hammered 9–0.

The club have played in four finals, losing only the 1974 UEFA Cup Final against Feyenoord 4–2 over the two legs. Spurs' record in European finals is:

Year	Comp	Venue	Result
1963	European Cup Winners Cup	Rotterdam	Tottenham 5 Atletico Madrid 1
1972	UEFA Cup	H & A	Tottenham 3 Wolves 2 (agg)
1974	UEFA Cup	H & A	Tottenham 2 Feyenoord 4 (agg)
1984	UEFA Cup	H & A	Tottenham 2 Anderlecht 2 (agg)*

* Tottenham won 4–3 on pens

— IN A NON-LEAGUE OF THEIR OWN —

Tottenham Hotspur won the FA Cup in 1901 in one of the most famous triumphs in the history of the competition. A Southern League outfit at the time, Spurs became, and indeed remain, the only non-league side ever to win the FA Cup – a feat which is unlikely ever to be matched.

In the final of 1901 Spurs played northern giants Sheffield United, and there was far more than the pride of the two clubs at stake. At the time, clubs from the north of England, which had embraced professionalism early, were dominant, while the south's refusal to leave amateurism behind had condemned it to the football wilderness. The FA Cup had been monopolised by the north since Blackburn Olympic beat Kinnaird's Old Etonians in the 1883 final. Now Spurs had the chance to break the northern stranglehold.

Although Tottenham's first eleven comprised an Irishman, two Welshmen, five Scots, and three players from the north of England,

Londoners viewed the team as their own, and on April 27th thousands descended upon the south London suburb of Sydenham to see the final at the Crystal Palace. The official attendance on a bright, hot afternoon was 114,815, but many thousands more watched from any vantage point they could clamber upon.

The Blades went ahead after 11 minutes, and a carrier pigeon was despatched to Sheffield with the news. But the bird had barely taken wing when centre-forward Alexander 'Sandy' Brown equalised for Spurs. On 50 minutes Brown put Spurs ahead, but a minute later United equalised controversially. Spurs goalkeeper George Clawley fumbled a cross and the ball dropped just wide of the post. The linesman signalled a corner but, incredibly, with goal nets not yet invented, referee Arthur Kingscott signalled a goal – much to the anger of the Spurs fans. The game finished 2–2, setting up a replay at Bolton's Burnden Park one week later.

The controversy over 'the goal that never was' was fuelled by the fact that this was the first final to be filmed by movie camera. Across the country the newsreels clearly showed the ball had gone wide of the post, with the unfortunate Mr Kingscott from Derbyshire becoming the first referee to be caught out by the camera.

Requests to the private rail companies for cheap rates to ferry Tottenham's fans north to the replay were refused, as were similar requests from Yorkshire. This, combined with major works at Bolton station, meant that a mere 30,000 saw the replay.

Despite this lack of support, Spurs came back from a goal down to win 3–1, thanks to goals from John Cameron, Tom Smith and Brown. It was, said *The Times*, 'the best football seen in the final tie for a long time' and the scenes of joy in London's streets when the news came through were compared to those which had greeted news of the relief of Mafeking a year before. Thousands turned out to welcome the south's heroes when they returned to London.

— HOT SHOT GREAVSIE —

The legendary Jimmy Greaves holds the record for scoring the most goals for Tottenham in competitive matches.

In nine years between 1961 and 1970, Greaves netted an amazing 266 goals in 379 appearances – a goals-to-game ratio of 70%. In the league, Greaves scored 220 goals in 321 games, while in the cups he was even more prolific. In the FA Cup, he bagged 32 in 36, with five in eight League Cup appearances and nine in 14 European games. Such was his value to the team he never once started as a sub.

Bobby Smith, with 208 goals in 317 games between 1955 and 1964 (a ratio of 66%), and Martin Chivers, with 174 goals in 355 games between 1968 and 1976 (47%) are second and third in the all-time Spurs goal-scoring charts.

— COMPLETING THE DOUBLE —

During the famous 1960/61 season, the championship-winning Tottenham Hotspur side won the FA Cup with the following sequence of games:

Date	Round	Result	Scorers
Jan 7th	3rd	Tottenham 3 Charlton Athletic 2	Allen 2, Dyson
Jan 28th	4th	Tottenham 5 Crewe 1	Mackay, Jones, Smith R, Allen, Dyson
Feb 18th	5th	Aston Villa 0 Tottenham 2	Jones, Neil og
Mar 4th	6th	Sunderland 1 Tottenham 1	Jones
Mar 8th	6th (replay)	Tottenham 5 Sunderland 0	Mackay, Smith R, Allen, Dyson 2
Mar 18th	S/F (Villa Park)	Tottenham 3 Burnley 0	Jones, Smith R 2
May 6th	Final (Wembley)	Tottenham 2 Leicester City 0	Smith R, Dyson

Danny Blanchflower lifts the 1961 FA Cup which secured the historic Double

— CHELSEA BLUES —

As supporters of West London's nouveau riche side never tire of telling their Spurs counterparts, before the start of the 2006/07 season Tottenham had not beaten Chelsea in the league for 16 years.

Goals from David Howells and Gary Lineker propelled Spurs to a 2–1 win at Stamford Bridge on February 10th 1990 on the last occasion the cockerel crowed against Chelsea in the league. After that it was a case of ifs, buts and maybes and the occasional thrashing – 32 games in all – until Aaron Lennon's strike in November 2006 finally ended the hoodoo. However, 16 major trophies to Chelsea's 13 tells another story, as do recollections of the following game:

Spurs 5, Chelsea 1
League Cup semi final second leg
January 23rd 2002
Glenn Hoddle's finest moment as Tottenham manager halted the hoodoo with Tottenham's first home win over Chelsea in all competitions for 15 years. Once Steffen Iversen gave Spurs the lead there was no going back and further strikes from Tim Sherwood, Teddy Sheringham, Simon Davies and Sergei Rebrov sent the visitors packing. The match became known as the 'Arfa 'Arfa game after this ditty was sung to the Chelsea fans as they slunk away from White Hart Lane:

> 'Who put the ball in Chelsea's net?
> 'Arfa, 'Arfa
> Who put the ball in Chelsea's net?
> Arfa Tottenham
> Half of Tot-tenham'
> [To the tune of *Camptown Races*]

— SING WHEN YOU'RE WINNING —

To mark their achievement in reaching the 1967 FA Cup Final, the Spurs team cut an LP to go with their cup final single *Glory Glory Hallelujah*. Recorded at EMI's famous Abbey Road studios in St John's Wood, the LP featured songs such as *Hello Dolly* and *The Bells Are Ringing*. Other tracks included:

Song	'Artist'
Bye Bye Blackbird	Terry Venables
Strollin'	Jimmy Greaves
I Belong To Glasgow	Dave Mackay, Jimmy Robertson, Alan Gilzean
Maybe It's Because I'm A Londoner	Alan Mullery, Frank Saul, Cyril Knowles, Eddie Clayton,
When Irish Eyes Are Smiling	Pat Jennings, Joe Kinnear, Mike England (!)

Incredibly, given this glittering array of showbiz talent, the LP failed to budge The Beatles' mega-hit *Sgt. Pepper's Lonely Hearts Club Band* from the top of the charts.

— EUROPEAN ADVENTURES —

Spurs have a distinguished record in Europe and midweek European games at White Hart Lane, played under floodlights, have always meant something special, providing the club with some of its finest achievements and most unforgettable contests.

Despite narrowly failing to qualify for the Champions League in 2005/06, Tottenham are still one of the most successful British clubs, with three trophy wins compared to Liverpool's eight and Manchester United's three – a better showing than the likes of Arsenal, Leeds United, Chelsea, West Ham, Nottingham Forest and the two Glasgow clubs.

The 2007/08 UEFA Cup campaign is the 15th time Spurs have competed in the UEFA-sanctioned competitions. This excludes the Intertoto Cup, in which Spurs have competed just once. The complete list of Spurs' European campaigns is:

Year	Competition	Progress
1961/62	European Cup	Semi-finalists (Lost 4–3 on aggregate to Benfica)
1962/63	European Cup Winners Cup	Winners (Beat Atletico Madrid 5–1 in final)
1963/64	European Cup Winners Cup	Second Round (Lost 6–3 on aggregate to Man Utd)
1967/68	European Cup Winners Cup	Second round (Lost on away goals to Olympique Lyonnais, aggregate score 4–4)
1971/72	UEFA Cup	Winners (Beat Wolverhampton Wanderers 3–2 on aggregate in the final)
1972/73	UEFA Cup	Semi-finalists (Lost on away goals to Liverpool, 2–2 on aggregate)
1973/74	UEFA Cup	Finalists (Lost 4–2 on aggregate to Feyenoord)
1981/82	European Cup Winners Cup	Semi-finalists (Lost 2–1 on aggregate to Barcelona)
1982/83	European Cup Winners Cup	Second round (Lost 5–2 on aggregate to Bayern Munich)

1983/84	UEFA Cup	Winners
		(Won 4–3 on penalties v
		Anderlecht, 2–2 on aggregate)
1984/85	UEFA Cup	Quarter-finalists
		(Lost 1–0 on aggregate to
		Real Madrid)
1991/92	European Cup	Quarter-finalists
	Winners Cup	(Lost 1–0 on aggregate
		to Feyenoord)
1999/2000	UEFA Cup	Second round
		(Lost 2–1 on aggregate to
		Kaiserslauten)
2006/07	UEFA Cup	Quarter-finalists
		(Lost 4–3 on aggregate to Sevilla)

— THE IMPORTANCE OF BEING EDGAR —

Signed on a free transfer from Inter Milan in August 2005, Edgar 'The Pitbull' Davids was arguably one of Tottenham's most important signings in the last decade, valued as much for his importance off the pitch as on it.

The Dutch international and former Champions League-winning Ajax, Milan, and Juventus midfielder brought a will to win, dedication on the training ground and a degree of professionalism that rubbed off on to his youthful teammates, and helped Spurs towards their highest league finish in 17 years.

Famed for his dreadlocks and protective sunglasses to offset the serious eye condition glaucoma, Davids is also rarely short of an opinion.

"When I was a young kid, we used to listen to Bob Marley's music a lot and I still feel that great vibe. He put all his heart and soul in his music and it's so important even today to do that at work or at school, basically with anything you do. One love."

"I feel blessed to be part of one of the most beautiful inventions known to mankind: Football."

"A lot has been said and written about me. Most of it misses the point. They just don't know. Well I can tell you this: it's the drive within. If anything, I start all over every time I come out of that tunnel and I never ever underestimate my opponent."

"I hope from now on the entire Spurs squad will manage to keep their head cool and get the most out of our effort every single match. The

Barclays Premiership is not about "should have beens": it's about complete dedication and maximum result."

"My motto is: real men don't dive."

"Gay players in the Premiership. I don't get what the big fuss is all about 'cause I couldn't care less. For those who are bothered by this: I think you should try and look for some professional help so that you can avoid any tragic misunderstandings."

"I miss the smell of a freshly cut pitch minutes before a match. The sound of football shoes clicking away impatiently in the crowded tunnel."

"There are some things about Tottenham Hotspur as a club that I really appreciate. Besides from being a football club with a great history, it's also a very social club with its feet planted firmly in society."

Dutch master: Edgar Davids

— AND SO THIS IS CHRISTMAS —

Just as turkeys don't like Christmas, the cockerel has rarely strutted its stuff over the festive period.

In the 95 Christmas programmes Spurs have participated in since joining the league, they have achieved an average of 3.83 points per Christmas – taking 364 points from the 718 on offer. In the 15 seasons since the Premiership started, Spurs have taken four points from 12 on four occasions, and four from nine on a further four.

The best Christmas in the Premiership came in 1994/95, when Spurs went unbeaten to claim 10 points from 12, only a 0–0 home draw against Crystal Palace taking the shine off a festive programme rounded off nicely by a 1–0 victory over Arsenal on January 2nd. Spurs also went unbeaten in 2004/05 when two wins and two draws secured eight points.

The team fared little better when the top division was the plain old First, averaging between four and seven points back to 1981/82, the first season when the three points for a win rule was introduced.

The longest Christmas unbeaten run came between 1972/73 and 1974/75, with five draws and two wins in the seven matches played. Maximum points have been won on only three occasions, the last time being the Double-winning season of 1960/61. The Christmases of 1952 and 1943 were also happy ones, with Spurs winning all the points on offer.

On the most special Christmas Day of all, December 25th 1911, Spurs beat Woolwich Arsenal 5–0. Now that's a Christmas cracker!

— CHAMPAGNE ON ICE —

Tottenham's record win in Europe is the 15–1 aggregate victory over Keflavik of Iceland in September 1971.

In the first leg in Reykjavik, Spurs won 6–1 with goals from Gilzean (3), Coates and Mullery (2). A hardy 200 supporters had travelled from England to watch them, forming part of the 10,000 strong crowd which packed into the tiny stadium nestled at the foot of the mountains. Back in the somewhat less picturesque surroundings of White Hart Lane for the return leg, Chivers (3), Perryman, Coates, Knowles, Gilzean (2) and Holder secured a club record 9–0 victory in Europe (equalling the score in the FA Cup victory over Worksop in 1923 and the league defeat of Bristol Rovers in 1978).

— CAPTAIN KID —

On September 28th 1972, 21-year-old Steve Perryman became Tottenham's youngest captain, leading the side out in a UEFA Cup second leg tie against Lyn Oslo at White Hart Lane. Perryman only found out that he was wearing the skipper's armband at 6.30pm on the night of the game, when Bill Nicholson walked into the dressing-room to announce that club captain Martin Peters had failed a fitness test. Happily, Stevie's big night went well, Spurs winning 6–0.

— CAN WE PLAY YOU EVERY OTHER WEEK? —

Tottenham's most favoured opponents are Aston Villa. In 143 league and cup games against the Midlanders (up to the start of the 2007/08 season), Spurs have prevailed on 59 occasions. However, Villa have themselves won 53 times, so perhaps Spurs would only like to play them every other week!

— MACNAMARA'S BAND —

The old Irish musical hall song first became associated with Spurs in the late fifties and early sixties when one of the world's greatest ever Irishmen, Danny Blanchflower, played for the team. The song was played as the team ran out for years, and a snippet can still be heard at the start of the second half at White Hart Lane.

Written by Seamus O'Connor and John J Stamford in 1917, the song has been recorded by artists including Bing Crosby and The Jesters, Connie Francis and Spike Jones and his City Slickers. In 1997 The Evergreens released a version on an Irish folk compilation called *The Wild Rover*, and it's this version that made it on to the compilation CD *We Are Tottenham* (Cherry Red records) in 2003.

A version of one of the verses was adapted by Spurs fans and has been sung at matches for some years. It goes:

Oh the cockerel crows, the whistle blows, and now we're in the game
It's up to you, you Lilywhites, to live up to your name
Oh there's other teams from other towns and some are great and small
The famous Tottenham Hotspur are the greatest of them all

Lalalala lalalalala lalalalalalala . . .

— DOUBLE YOUR NUMBER —

Some impressive numbers from the 1960/61 Double season:

1: The number of penalties Spurs conceded
1: The number of cautions picked up by Spurs players
54,588: the average home gate for league and cup games
65,930: the biggest home gate of the season (v West Ham, Div 1)
33: number of goals scored by Bobby Smith in league and cup
2: the number of games – out of 49 – in which Spurs failed to score
0: the number of clubs who had won the Double in the 20th Century, prior to the 1960/61 season

— THE FIRST MANAGER —

Tottenham's first manager was Frank Brettell. Brettell was the first manager worthy of the name; hitherto teams were run on a fairly ad hoc basis by players, secretaries, presidents and various committee members. He was given the post of secretary-manager in February 1898, and began work in March. He'd previously held the same position for Bolton Wanderers, had been a player with Everton and a reporter for the *Liverpool Mercury*. He was in charge for a year, during which time he brought a large number of Bolton players south. He took charge for 63 games, overseeing 37 wins, 12 draws and 14 defeats. He resigned on February 8th 1899 after Portsmouth offered him more money.

— WINNING STREAKS —

Tottenham's eight consecutive wins in the 2006/07 UEFA Cup, before the 2–1 quarter-final first-leg defeat to Sevilla, took the team to within one win of the competition record set by Borussia Moenchengladbach in the 1974/75 tournament.

In fact, only four teams have bettered Tottenham's record of consecutive wins in Europe, including the mouth-wateringly-named Germans. In the 1992/93 Champions League, AC Milan won ten games on the trot, while in 2002/03, Barcelona racked up 11 wins in a row in the same competition. Dutch masters Ajax also notched up 11 wins in a row – although their record was set over two competitions, the 1986/87 and 1987/88 Cup Winners' Cups.

— SPURS LEGENDS: BILL NICHOLSON —

The legendary Bill Nicholson

In choosing who is the most significant figure in Tottenham's long and illustrious history, there is really only one candidate – Bill Nicholson.

In an association with the club that spanned eight decades, Nicholson was a player, manager, chief scout, president and legend. His influence cannot be overstated: prior to his arrival, the club had lifted two major trophies. By the time he stepped down as boss in 1974, another nine had been added to the honours list. His achievements set the standards that all other Tottenham sides have sought to emulate, not just to win football matches but to do so in style.

Nicholson was born in Scarborough on January 26th 1919, into a family of nine with a father who was a groom and horse cab driver. Despite doing well at school, in common with virtually every boy of his age and class, Nicholson had to forego further education and went to work at 16, in his case at a local laundry.

A good if unspectacular footballer, playing for Scarborough's Young Liberals side, he was identified by the Tottenham scouting network in the area before the club's chief scout, Ben Ives, paid a visit to check. Suitably impressed, Ives recommended a month's trial and after a spell with the nursery side Northfleet, Nicholson turned professional at 18.

War interrupted Nicholson's career, but his service as an army PT instructor helped to develop his abilities to train and manage players. Picking up where he left off in 1946, the de-mobbed Sergeant Nicholson became a mainstay of the Tottenham side until 1954, initially as a combative centre-half, then as right-half. During that period he won an England cap, scoring after just 19 seconds in a 5–2 victory over Portugal in 1951, but never played for the national side again, despite many at the time feeling he was the best player in his position.

Playing under Arthur Rowe as a key member of Tottenham's 1951 title-winning team was vital in Nicholson's development as a manager and he became a passionate disciple of the idea that football was not just about winning, but winning well.

In an era of post-war austerity and conservative attitudes on the football pitch, this was a philosophy few others shared. The football establishment put their parochial faith in the old English virtues of physical effort and unimaginative application.

Embarrassing defeats for the national side at the hands of Hungary exposed such shortsightedness, and with it Nicholson's time had come. He became head coach at White Hart Lane in 1955 and gained further education and inspiration working with England manager Walter Winterbottom. When Jimmy Anderson resigned, Nicholson stepped up to become Spurs boss and officially took up the managerial reigns at midday on Saturday October 11th 1958.

His first game in charge gave a perfect illustration of what was to come, as Spurs thumped Everton 10–4. "We don't score ten every week, you know," said Tommy Harmer to his new manager as the team left the pitch to a standing ovation, but the football Nicholson's teams subsequently played proved to be just as thrilling.

Nicholson had inherited some outstanding players – Danny Blanchflower, Maurice Norman, Bobby Smith, Cliff Jones, Terry

Dyson and Terry Medwin among them – but proved to be a shrewd operator in the transfer market as well, signing the likes of Dave Mackay, John White and Bill Brown. Nicholson was no desk-bound mover and shaker, however. He was first and foremost a coach, who spent as little time as possible in the office and as much as he could out on the training pitch (including the indoor facility he demanded should be built behind the West Stand so that the players could hone their skills whatever the weather).

Ably assisted by Harry Evans and later Eddie Baily, Nicholson created what many fans and pundits alike still regard as the greatest-ever English club side. They carried all before them in 1960/61, smashed records and established a new benchmark for the game in Britain. In the season after, Spurs nearly became the first British side to win the European Cup, defeated in controversial circumstances in the semi-final by Benfica. (See *Classic Matches* 4, page 103) Compensation was to come in the 1962/63 season when Spurs won the European Cup Winners' Cup.

After such dazzling highs, it was almost inevitable that Nicholson would struggle to match them, but he still produced another two great sides, winning the FA Cup for a third time in 1967 and fashioning the early 1970s team that won the UEFA Cup and the League Cup (twice). By 1974, however, disenchanted with the negativity of modern football, the demands of the media and the blight of hooliganism, he resigned.

But Nicholson continued to be a major part of the White Hart Lane scene, returning as chief scout after a brief spell in the same role at West Ham, then as club president. A warm and sincere man, he was forever approachable to supporters, even turning up for a fans' protest against the sacking of then manager and co-owner Terry Venables in 1993. He was a regular at Spurs matches well into old age, until his death on October 23rd 2004, at the age of 85.

Bill Nicholson CBE never got the knighthood he deserved, but the lack of suitable 'official' recognition did nothing to diminish the esteem he is still held in by everyone connected with Spurs. The thoroughfare that leads off from Tottenham High Road to the stadium is named Bill Nicholson Way; it's the name of a road but it sums up the philosophy of the club itself – the Spurs way is the Bill Nick way.

— TOP OF THE POPS —

Popular songs adapted by the White Hart Lane faithful:

Chim Chim Cheree, Dick van Dyke and Julie Andrews (1964)
('Chim Chimenee, Chim Chimenee, Chim Chim Cheroo, Nayim from 50 yards, Belletti from two'.)

Yellow Submarine, The Beatles (1966)
('Number one, is Robbie Keane, number two, is Robbie Keane, number three, is Robbie Keane . . .' etc, 'We all dream of a team of Robbie Keanes, a team of Robbie Keanes, a team of Robbie Keanes . . .')

Sailing, Rod Stewart (1972)
('We are Tottenham, We are Tottenham, Super Tottenham, From the Lane . . .')

Seasons in the Sun, Terry Jacks (1974)
('We had joy, we had fun, we had Arsenal on the run, but the joy didn't last, 'cos the f***ers ran too fast.')

Hersham Boys, Sham 69 (1979)
('Tottenham boys, Tottenham boys, laced-up boots and corduroys.')

No Limits, 2 UnLimited (1993)
('Noé Noé, Noé Noé Noé Noé, Noé Noé Noé Noé, Noé Noé, He's Noé Pamarot.')

Wonderwall, Oasis (1996)
('All the runs that Ronnie does are winding, And all the goals that Ronnie scores are blinding, There are many things that I would like to say to you, But I don't know how, But maybe, you're gonna be the one that saves me, And after all, you're my Rosenthal.')

— HOME COMFORT —

The disappointment of the eight-minute collapse at the start of the UEFA Cup quarter final second leg against Sevilla, in which Spurs conceded two goals and were effectively dumped out of the competition, was tempered slightly by the fightback to a 2–2 draw which preserved a proud record. Of the 55 home games Spurs have played in Europe, only one has been lost. Even that was thanks to a Steve Perryman own goal against Real Madrid in the 1983/84 UEFA Cup. Spurs have won 45 of their European home ties at White Hart Lane, with nine draws.

— THE HOME OF FOOTBALL —

Spurs played their first games on Tottenham Marshes, an area of common land between the Great Eastern Railway and the River Lea, in 1882. The club established a regular pitch at the Park Lane end of the Marshes a year later.

But as the number of spectators grew, sometimes reaching in excess of 4,000 watching games on what was still a piece of public ground, it became more and more difficult to control the increasingly boisterous crowds. The club needed an enclosed pitch, and in 1888 found one for hire just off Northumberland Park, a street which ran off the High Road. The pitch was also used by a local side called Foxes FC, and in the summer was used for tennis. Spurs agreed to pay £17 a year for its use.

The first match there was played in early September 1888, a reserve game against Stratford St Johns. It's perhaps an indicator of things to come that while the result is not recorded, the takings of 17 shillings 85p were. Grandstands were raised at Northumberland Park as football's mass popularity took hold, with a record crowd of 14,000 turning up on April 29th 1899 for the visit of Woolwich Arsenal. Unfortunately, that was at least twice what the ground could hold, and many spectators were injured in the crush. It was clear a new ground was needed.

Fortunately a chance presented itself when an undeveloped plot of land called Beckwith's Nursery, one of the many patches of ground in Tottenham used at the time to grow flowers for the London market, became available. The plot was situated next to the White Hart pub on Tottenham High Road, and owned by the brewers Charrington, which had purchased the land with the intention of building houses to provide custom for the pub. Instead, Charrington agreed to lease the ground to Spurs, asking only for a guaranteed attendance of 1,000 at first team games and 500 at the reserves. The landlord, whose previous pub had been near Millwall's ground, knew the custom a local football team would bring, and the brewers also secured an agreement that the club would only serve Charrington beers.

The new 30,000 capacity ground was formally opened on September 4th 1899, with Spurs beating Notts County 4–1 in a friendly in front of 5,000 people. Although early favourites for names included Percy Park, Gilpin Park and the exceedingly dull High Road Ground, the stadium was never formally named, and simply became known as White Hart Lane.

— AND IF YOU KNOW YOUR HISTORY —

Countess Judith holds Tottenham of the King. It is assessed at 5 hides. There is land for 10 ploughs. . . There are two Frenchmen on 1 hide and woodland for 500 pigs. In all it is worth £25.15s and 3 ounces of gold. Earl Waltheof held this manor.

Entry for Tottenham in The Domesday Book, 1086

Nearly a thousand years later, Earl Waltheof, Countess Judith, the two Frenchmen and several hundred pigs would find Tottenham a somewhat different place. Swallowed up by the 19th century expansion of London, Tottenham the area has been made famous by its football club, but there have been some notable events and characters along the way. Here's a potted history of the medieval village that gave the world its finest football club.

Middle ages: Toteham, or 'homestead of the man called Totta', first settled in the 11th century near the old Roman road Ermine Street. Parish boundary established in 1300.

Tudor times: The area becomes a popular leisure spot for well-to-do Londoners, drawn to the local hunting grounds. King Henry VIII is a visitor and stays at Bruce Castle (the manor house of Sir William Compton, squire to the king's bedchamber).

17th century: Tottenham gets a mention in Izaak Walton's *The Compleat Angler*, portraying the area as something of a rural beauty spot.

19th century: Sir Rowland Hill, who developed Britain's postal system sets up home at Bruce Castle.

The arrival of the railways, industrialisation and the development of the nearby River Lea and New River begin the evolution of Tottenham from quiet middle-class backwater into bustling London suburb for the urban working-class. Tottenham becomes part of the London Borough of Haringey:

1882: Still semi rural and surrounded by market gardens, Tottenham gets its very own football club.

1909: Two Latvian 'anarchist' armed robbers hold up a wages clerk at a local factory. Pursued by police, a gun battle ensues, leaving four dead (including a boy of 10) and 21 wounded. The 'Tottenham Outrage' as it was dubbed is later turned into a hit silent film.

World War II: The area is bombed and later hit by V1 and V2 rockets.

1985: The Broadwater Farm Housing estate, within sight of the stadium, suffers a night of serious rioting during which PC Keith Blakelock is murdered.

— TOP OF THE LEAGUE, TEMPORARILY —

In season 1925/26 the club topped the league for the first time in their history – but eventually finished in 15th place after losing eight of their last 13 games.

— SPURS SCOOP THE WORLD —

It cost £1,500 to buy Keith Burkinshaw a plane ticket to Buenos Aires in June 1978, but it was money well spent as Burkinshaw returned to London to announce a deal that stunned the football world.

During that summer's World Cup, fans around the globe had marvelled at Argentina's World Cup winners. On Thursday June, 29th three days after the host nation beat Holland 3–1 in the final, Bill Nicholson's phone rang. The former manager still had an office across the corridor from Burkinshaw, and midway through the call he laid the receiver on his desk and hurried across to haul the Spurs boss out of a board meeting. He told Burkinshaw that his friend Harry Haslam, the Sheffield United manager, was on the line with the news that Osvaldo Ardiles and Ricardo Villa were available for sale.

Haslam was something of an expert on Argentine players thanks to his Argentine coach, the unfortunately-named Oscar Arce. Through Arce, Haslam had a connection to Antonio Rattin, who was the players' agent. Rattin was a former Argentina captain whose previous claim to fame was to have become the first man ever to be sent off at Wembley during the 1966 World Cup quarter-final against England, the Argentines' brutal play leading the normally reserved Alf Ramsey to brand them 'animals' after the game. Rattin evidently harboured no grudge against the English, however, for he agreed to act for Burkinshaw.

The Tottenham boss went straight back into the board meeting and asked for immediate approval to fly to Buenos Aires to complete the deal. Despite the exorbitant cost of the plane ticket, the board agreed. Then Burkinshaw called the Department of Employment to check that a work permit could be obtained. It could.

The flight was due to leave on Friday evening, and Burkinshaw's intention was to sign Ardiles. At the last minute, news that Arsenal manager Terry Neill was also planning to be on the same flight came through. Burkinshaw was relieved when it turned out that Neill wasn't interested. It's not known if Arsenal's board rejected the deal, although Neill maintains he didn't need Ardiles or Villa because he already had Graham Rix and Liam Brady.

The lure of playing in Spurs' new Admiral kit was too much to resist for Villa and Ardiles

The Tottenham manager arrived in Buenos Aires on Saturday morning and checked into the Hotel Libertador. A few hours later he met Ardiles, struck up an instant rapport, and a deal was agreed within 20 minutes. Ardiles then shocked his new manager. "He told me he had a friend, Ricardo Villa, who also wanted to play in England. Could he come too?" remembers Burkinshaw.

Burkinshaw had secured boardroom approval because Ardiles

would cost £350,000, a bargain price but one that was attractive to the players' debt-ridden club Huracan. But he didn't know much about Villa, who played for Racing Club and had made just two substitute appearances for Argentina in the finals, but what he did know was that he could secure two World Cup winners for £700,000 – a snip considering that Manchester United had just paid £450,000 for defender Gordon McQueen.

Back in England, Tottenham chairman Sidney Wale was about to sit down to his Sunday lunch when the phone rang. It was Burkinshaw, asking if he could sign Villa too. "He wanted an answer straight away," remembers Wale. "I did some quick mental arithmetic . . . how much the bank would allow us on overdraft . . . how much extra we could raise from season ticket sales . . . and I thought, we'll take a chance. We were both putting our heads on the chopping block. It was a big gamble to take, but . . . it was the best decision I ever made." Villa later revealed he thought he would be going to Arsenal, and that he was simply travelling to London to accompany his friend!

Spurs paid cash on the nail, and not a word came out about the deal until Burkinshaw was ready to announce it on Friday July 7th. It was, wrote the *Daily Mail*'s Jeff Powell, 'The most sensational deal in British football history'.

— SOME SUPPORTERS ARE ON THE PITCH —

How's this for a line-up? A top-quality team of Spurs-supporting players who never played for the club.

1. **Alex Stepney** (Manchester United)
2. **Matt Taylor** (Portsmouth)
3. **Chris Powell** (Charlton)
4. **Des Walker** (Nottm Forest, Sampdoria, Sheffield Wednesday)
5. **Ken Monkou** (Chelsea and Southampton)
6. **Roy Keane** (Nottm Forest, Manchester United and Celtic)
7. **Michael Thomas** (Arsenal and Liverpool)
8. **Dennis Bergkamp** (Ajax, Inter Milan and Arsenal)
9. **Dwight Yorke** (Aston Villa, Manchester United, Blackburn Rovers)
10. **Matt Le Tissier** (Southampton)
11. **Eidur Gudjohnsen** (Bolton, Chelsea and Barcelona)

Subs: Chris Bart-Williams (Nottingham Forest), Barry Hayles (Fulham), Jason Roberts (Blackburn Rovers), Lomano Lua Lua (Portsmouth), Marlon Harewood (West Ham)

— CLASSIC MATCHES 1: GREAVSIE MAGIC —

Tottenham 5	Manchester United 1
Johnson	Charlton
Clayton	
Greaves	
Gilzean	
Robertson	

October 16th 1965: Division One
White Hart Lane
Att: 58,051

Forget England in 1966, Manchester United winning the European Cup two years later and even, for a moment, the exploits of the Spurs Double side of 1960/61. The greatest games of the swinging sixties were the Division One clashes between Spurs and Manchester United in the 1965/66 season, each side triumphing 5–1 on their home patch.

Two goals from Denis Law and a Bobby Charlton volley helped United to a convincing victory at Old Trafford in December 1965, avenging the reverse Spurs had inflicted at White Hart Lane back in October. Spurs raced to a 4–0 advantage in that game, capped by arguably the greatest ever goal scored by a Tottenham player. Jimmy Greaves picked up the ball in his own half of the pitch, waltzed past four United defenders and bamboozled goalkeeper Dunne as he calmly rounded him and coolly passed the ball home, sending the crowd and *Match of the Day* commentator Kenneth Wolstenhome into a frenzy. Classic Greaves, classic Spurs.

— NIGHT OF A THOUSAND SPURS —

The Spurs v Blackburn game on 10th May 2007 was Sky TV's 1,000th live Premiership match. Up until the start of the 2007/08 season, Tottenham's record live on Sky was:

Played	Won	Drawn	Lost	For	Against
105	34	30	44	145	160

— LIGHTNING LEDLEY —

Spurs star Ledley King set a new record for the fastest-ever Premiership goal when he scored Tottenham's first in a 3–3 draw with Bradford City on December 9th 2000 at Valley Parade. King's strike came after just 10 seconds, a feat equalled by Alan Shearer in Newcastle United's game against Manchester City on January 18th 2003.

— SUPERSTITIOUS MINDS —

Traditionally, the Spurs coach won't pass under a railway bridge when there is a train passing overhead. The reasons for this particular superstition are lost in the mists of time, but others are more attributable, as with this selection of player hang-ups. Some may scoff but, as these footballers will testify, when it comes to superstitions it's best not to tempt fate.

Clive Allen: Would never score in the pre-match warm up. The ritual worked in the 1986/87 season when he scored 49 goals in all competitions.

Martin Chivers: A player who occasionally exasperated as well as thrilled, his critics' frustration would only have been magnified by Chivers' rather confused superstition. The striker initially opted to take the field minus his false teeth – but then reversed the habit. "I can't decide which brings good or bad luck," he said.

Gary Lineker: Would wear the same kit if he had performed well in the previous game, always changed his shirt in the second half if he hadn't scored in the first, and would wear the same shirt if he had scored. If he went on a bad run, Lineker would have his hair cut, which is probably why his coiffure rarely altered during his three seasons at Tottenham.

Mark Falco: "It's bad luck to discuss superstitions," discussed the striker in 1985.

— UNITED NATIONS —

Tottenham's 1–1 draw at Aston Villa on September 17th 2005 was the first time in the club's history that Spurs started (and finished) with 11 full internationals. The line-up was:

Paul Robinson (England)
Anthony Gardner (England)
Ledley King (England)
Lee Young-Pyo (South Korea)
Paul Stalteri (Canada)
Michael Carrick (England)
Teemu Tainio (Finland)
Andy Reid (Republic of Ireland)
Jermaine Jenas (England)
Jermain Defoe (England)
Grzegorz Rasiak (Poland)

Subs used:
Noureddine Naybet (Morocco)
Robbie Keane (Republic of Ireland)

— SPURS LEGENDS: PAUL GASCOIGNE —

Paul Gascoigne played for Spurs for only three seasons, but rarely has a player made such an impact at the club in such a short space of time . . . on and off the pitch.

Gazza was signed from Newcastle United in July 1988 for the then British record fee of £2m, as Terry Venables started to rebuild Spurs in earnest following his own arrival from Barcelona a year before. He was the most talented young player of his generation and his signing represented a significant coup for Spurs, given the interest of other clubs including Manchester United, whose manager Alex Ferguson had been informed by Gascoigne that he was ready to move to Old Trafford. But Spurs offered more money – £1,500 per week basic compared to the £250 a week on offer to re-sign for Newcastle – and with former Newcastle teammate Glenn Roeder and Spurs winger Chris Waddle recommending a move to London, Gazza put pen to paper on a four-year deal at the Lane.

With a perfect sense of comic timing the fixture computer drew out Newcastle as the opponents for Gascoigne's Spurs debut. At St James' Park on September 3rd 1988, in a 2–2 draw, Gascoigne's reputation as an enthusiastic consumer of sweets caught up with him and the home fans showered Mars bars on to the pitch.

Over the next three years, the fun-loving Gascoigne provided ample evidence of his supreme skills without ever quite becoming the world-beater his talent promised. He played 112 times for Spurs in all competitions, scoring 33 goals. Following the 1990 World Cup he emerged as the superstar of English football's renaissance, but injuries, the Tottenham team's relative lack of progress and off-field problems for player and club left a sense of what might have been rather than the warm glow of satisfaction with what actually happened.

By 1991, with Tottenham on the verge of bankruptcy, Gascoigne was touted for a big-money move abroad, eventually signing for Lazio in May 1992 for a record fee of £5.5m, quite possibly rescuing Spurs from financial ruin. If his departure left supporters downhearted, his parting gift was a generous one, as he almost single-handedly steered Tottenham towards their eighth FA Cup triumph.

Undoubtedly, his finest moment in a Spurs shirt came in the epic semi-final against Arsenal at Wembley, with the Spurs talisman scoring one of the cup's greatest-ever goals to set his side on their way to a famous 3–1 win (See *Classic Matches 5*, page 119). In the final against Nottingham Forest, Gascoigne's reckless tackle on Gary Charles led to him being stretchered off in agony. The cruciate ligament injury Gazza sustained almost ended his career, but after a year-long rehabilitation he bid London farewell and left for Rome.

— GAZZA ON GAZZA —

"I'm getting loyalty discounts from my rehab clinic."

"I never make predictions, and I never will."

"I've had 14 bookings this season – 8 of which were my fault, but 7 of which were disputable."

"Because of the booking, I will miss the Holland game – if selected."

"It was a big relief off my shoulder."

"I'm enjoying every day. I've tried everything: duck's head, chicken's head, chicken's feet and bats and hopefully, if I keep that up, I'll be flying."
On his time in Chinese football

— WE'VE GOT THEM SINGING THE BLUES —

Legend has it that, as a thank you for Spurs letting Arsenal use White Hart Lane during World War II (Highbury was requisitioned by the government), the Arsenal board promised, and still keep the promise, that somewhere on every Arsenal kit – even if it's just the badge – there is a little bit of blue . . .

— PRATT'S THE WAY TO DO IT—

After an 8–2 thrashing at Derby in October 1976, manager Keith Burkinshaw dragged the squad in for a training-ground inquest, asking each player for his assessment. Keith Osgood said, "I let their man turn me for the second goal, otherwise I thought I was ok." Goalkeeper Barry Daines said, "A couple of them were my fault boss, but not the rest." Terry Naylor said, "I'm my own biggest critic boss, and I'd say if I thought I'd had a stinker." The rest of the players took it in turns to excuse their role in the rout, until attention turned to John Pratt. "Well," he said, "it looks like everyone else has had a blinder so I guess it must all be my f******* fault!"

— BADGE OF HONOUR —

It is one of the most distinctive images in club football – a strutting cockerel symbolising the confidence (and some might argue the cockiness) of the club. But where does the Spurs badge come from?

Prior to the adoption of the cockerel, Tottenham players sported various emblems, initially a large letter 'H' for Hotspur and later a Maltese cross. The origins of the latter are a matter of some dispute. It is possible that the close links between the infant club and local churches led to the players adopting the stylised Christian symbol (according to club rules of 1883, all members had to attend scripture classes at All Hallows Church once a week).

So why the cockerel? It all goes back to that man Harry Hotspur (See *What's in the Name?*, page 2) (again). Hotspur reputedly wore distinctive riding spurs, hence the nickname. The same went for fighting cockerels that were a feature of gambling dens of old. Inevitably, the link was drawn between the two and first the fighting spur and then the cockerel were adopted as the club's insignia.

It appears that the Spurs cockerel was used initially in printed material and then as the copper emblem that adorned the old West Stand in 1910, some 11 years before it first appeared on the team shirt.

Later badges added various other features, including rampant lions and symbols that represented the local area – a turreted tower for Bruce Castle and the seven elm trees that gave the Seven Sisters locale its name, for example. The club's Latin motto, 'Audere est facere', was also included on several versions of the shirt badge.

Early in 2006, the club redesigned the badge as part of a 'rebranding' exercise. In came a sleeker, sharper, altogether swishier cockerel (still with his spurs and standing on a handsome old-style laced football), out went the Latin motto, replaced instead with the English translation, 'To dare is to do'.

The makeover was generally well received by supporters, but the loss of the Latin disappointed a Dr Peter Jones, of the Friends of Classics organisation. "It strikes me as a shame to lose it," he said. "It seems pointless to me and sums up the contempt football clubs have for their fans. The point is that in the 19th century a Latin signature gave status and quality to a club. I suspect that football clubs now regard it as an anomaly, not as something that gives a status to it. A logo in another language is something of great importance."

— CHAMPIONS 1951 —

Division One

	P	W	D	L	F	A	Pts
1. Tottenham Hotspur	42	25	10	7	82	44	60
2. Manchester United	42	24	8	10	74	40	56
3. Blackpool	42	20	10	12	79	53	50
4. Newcastle United	42	18	13	11	62	53	49
5. Arsenal	42	19	9	14	73	56	47
6. Middlesbrough	42	18	11	13	76	65	47
7. Portsmouth	42	16	15	11	71	68	47
8. Bolton Wanderers	42	19	7	16	64	61	45
9. Liverpool	42	16	11	15	53	59	43
10. Burnley	42	14	14	14	48	43	42
11. Derby County	42	16	8	18	81	75	40
12. Sunderland	42	12	16	14	63	73	40
13. Stoke City	42	13	14	15	50	59	40
14. Wolverhampton Wanderers	42	15	8	19	74	61	38
15. Aston Villa	42	12	13	17	66	68	37
16. West Bromwich Albion	42	13	11	18	53	61	37
17. Charlton Athletic	42	14	9	19	63	80	37
18. Fulham	42	13	11	18	52	68	37
19. Huddersfield Town	42	15	6	21	64	92	36
20. Chelsea	42	12	8	22	53	65	32
21. Sheffield Wednesday	42	12	8	22	64	83	32
22. Everton	42	12	8	22	48	86	32

— SCORING FOR A TON OF FUN —

Tottenham's grand total of 104 goals in domestic and European competition during the 2006/07 season was the first time the club have hit the 100 mark since the 1986/87 season, when the total scored was 109.

— ANGELIC UPSTARTS —

The 1961 European Cup, first round, second leg tie between Spurs and Gornik was notable for the first outing of the Spurs anthem, *Glory Glory Hallelujah*. Its origins are still subject to some debate, but one theory is that the song stemmed from accusations from the Polish opposition that Spurs adopted a physical approach in the first game. This slight against Tottenham's good name hinged on a tackle from Dave Mackay on the Gornik left half Kowalski and led to claims that Super Spurs were 'no angels'.

In response, a group of Spurs fans dressed up as angels for the return leg and walked around the perimeter of the pitch before kick-off. Some nameless individual in the crowd joined in the fun by singing a few bars from *The Battle Hymn of the Republic*, the original song adopted by the Union forces in the American Civil War. *Glory Glory . . .* seemed so apt, not just for the religious connotations, but its pertinence in reflecting Tottenham's glorious style of football. And so a legend was, allegedly, born that night.

Today the song is still popular at White Hart Lane. It has been much copied by supporters of other clubs who replace 'Hallelujah' with the name of their team, but the true, unique, Spurs rendition retains the H word.

Glory Glory Hallelujah
Glory Glory Hallelujah
Glory Glory Hallelujah
And the Spurs go marching on

— ALL SAINTS —

John Chiedozie, Chris Hughton and Jermain Defoe have all starred for Tottenham; in addition, they were all pupils at St Bonaventure's School in Newham, East London. The school is barely a Tomas Repka hoof away from Upton Park, but the lure of the Lilywhite, 11 miles distant at White Hart Lane, has proved irresistible.

— FROM BULGARIA, WITH LOVE —

Tottenham fans have always taken a mercurial talent to their hearts and they found a new hero (and heartthrob for female fans) in 2006 when the club spent £10.9m on Bulgarian international striker, Dimitar Berbatov.

Signed from Bayer Leverkusen from under the noses of Manchester United and a host of other Champions' League clubs, Berbatov swiftly endeared himself to the White Hart Lane crowd – and neutrals – with a series of dazzling displays in the Lilywhite shirt, scoring 23 goals during his debut season in England, and was voted Tottenham's Player of the Season and scorer of goal of the season – a stunning all-round goal v Charlton at The Valley – by the supporters.

Berbatov facts:
For several games during the 2006/07 season, Berbatov wore an armband bearing the slogan 'You are not alone', referring to the cause of several Bulgarian medics imprisoned in Libya. They had been accused of deliberately spreading Aids, but Berbatov and his countrymen have consistently protested their innocence.

He learned English from watching the *Godfather* movie trilogy and is a dead ringer for the actor Andy Garcia who starred as a ruthless but handsome hitman in *Godfather III*.

He was voted into the 2007 Team of the Season by his fellow pros – one of only two players who didn't play for Manchester United or Chelsea.

In his own words:
"I am not a hero. I am an ordinary guy who plays football and entertains the fans."

"God gave me a talent and I try to show it."

"Hopefully this is the beginning of a wonderful partnership between me and Tottenham."
After scoring in the 3–1 win against Wigan.

— IN PRAISE OF BILL NICK —

"An inspiration."
Danny Blanchflower

"He was the complete manager."
Cliff Jones

"He never let us forget that we were out there to entertain the public. He was straight as a die, 100 per cent honest and 100 per cent Spurs."
Dave Mackay

"A fantastic tactician, superb coach and probably the best manager I've seen."
Alan Mullery

"Bill produced such a dazzling team at White Hart Lane that they won the Double and played the game in a way that was an object lesson to everybody."
Brian Clough

"Bill Nicholson was totally dedicated to this club. He's a fantastic man and it was an honour to serve under him."
Martin Peters

"To me he is all what Tottenham is about."
Martin Chivers

"He was a great man and a true gentleman. Bill had time for everyone – not just the players but the backroom staff and the supporters. He was a great ambassador for Tottenham Hotspur and for football."
Ralph Coates

"I was always in awe of him. He was the big man of Tottenham and the big man of football as far as I was concerned."
Steve Perryman

"Bill Nicholson is the name that is synonymous with Tottenham. His achievements, and the way in which he achieved them, will always be remembered by anyone with a Spurs connection."
Gary Mabbutt

"I have always had the deepest respect for Bill Nicholson as a person and as a manager."
Bill Shankly, Liverpool manager of the sixties and seventies (Shankly later described Nicholson's Spurs as 'cockney tap dancers')

"Bill was one of the greatest blokes, if not the greatest, that I have ever worked for."
Jimmy Greaves

"Bill was Mr Tottenham Hotspur and everything the club stands for emanated from Bill, who installed the foundations. He always remained totally dedicated to Spurs. He had presence, he knew what he wanted, he knew how his team should and would function. He established the traditions of Tottenham Hotspur Football Club."
Glenn Hoddle

— STATION TO STATION —

By 1932 Arsenal's Henry Norris had already masterminded his team's move from Plumstead to Highbury (See *Seeds of a Great Rivalry*, page 5) and the plundering of Tottenham's rightful place in the top flight of English football (although Spurs roared back into the top flight after just one season in spectacular style). But Norris wasn't finished yet.

The underground station beside Arsenal's ground had been open since 1906 and, as it stood on Gillespie Road, was entirely sensibly named Gillespie Road station. But Norris persuaded the transport authorities to change the name to Arsenal (Highbury Hill), securing a fantastic piece of publicity for his club. The brackets were, of course, gradually dropped and the residents of Gillespie Road remain saddled with this imposed name to this day, the only Underground Station in London named after a football club.

Even after Arsenal re-located to new premises on a converted rubbish tip in Holloway Road (no plans to rename the local underground station as yet), London Underground and the Mayor of London refused to reinstate the name of Gillespie Road, despite a vociferous campaign to do so and an online petition.

— ERIK THE FIRST —

Erik Thorstvedt was the first ever substitute in the Premier League, coming on for Ian Walker during Tottenham's 2–0 home defeat to Coventry on August 19th 1992.

Spurs' first Football League substitute was Roy Low, who replaced Derek Possee in a home match against Arsenal on September 11th 1965.

— CLASSIC MATCHES 2:
'WE'RE THE NORTH BANK TOTTENHAM' —

Spurs 3   **Wolves 0**
Crooks (2)
Villa

April 15th 1981: FA Cup semi-final replay
Highbury
Att: 52,539

'The best performance by a home side at Highbury all season' was the popular description of Tottenham's glorious thrashing of Wolves. Having been held to a 2–2 draw in the first game at Hillsborough thanks to referee Clive Thomas awarding Wolves a controversial late penalty, Spurs were determined to ensure nothing was left to chance in the replay. Their opponents cried foul over the choice of a venue so close to Tottenham and with some justification, for Highbury was transformed into White Hart Lane on an unforgettable night of thrilling football theatre.

Spurs simply annexed their deadly rivals' home patch. London N5 was a sea of blue and white, with flags and scarves hanging from windows and the local pubs heaving with Tottenham supporters. Inside the stadium Tottenham's overwhelming superiority in terms of numbers was even more marked with barely 5,000 Black Countrymen in attendance in a capacity crowd. Nothing – not even an attack by Arsenal fans who threw a few salvos of half-bricks into the North Bank from outside the ground – could dampen the atmosphere.

Roared on by the 'home' supporters, Spurs blew Wolves away with a double from Garth Crooks ending the contest by half time, the second engineered by a devastating Hoddle pass. Ricky Villa gave an indication of what lay in store in the final with the third, cutting in from the right before unleashing a vicious curling left-foot drive from nearly 25 yards.

Arguably, it was Tottenham's best performance of the season. That it came on Arsenal's home turf made it all the sweeter.

— THE PHILOSOPHY OF BILL NICK —

The words of the great Bill Nicholson:

"When not in possession, get into position."

"If you don't have to drag yourself off the field exhausted after 90 minutes, you can't claim to have done your best."

"The game has become tense and bound in fears. Everyone's trying to catch sparrows. I aim to recreate Mr [Arthur] Rowe's simple gospel: 'Make it plain, make it accurate, make it quick – especially quick.'"

"Spurs have got to be the best in the land, not the second best."

"If you don't win anything, you have had a bad season."

"Any player coming to Spurs, whether he's a big signing or just a ground staff boy, must be dedicated to the game and to the club. He must be prepared to work at his game. He must never be satisfied with his last performance, and he must hate losing."

"Intelligence doesn't make you a good footballer. Oxford and Cambridge would have the best sides if that were true. It's a football brain that matters and that doesn't usually go with an academic brain. In fact I prefer it when it doesn't. I prefer players not to be too good or clever at other things. It means they concentrate on football."

"Naturally I'm a Tottenham man. So far as football is concerned, it means almost everything, doesn't it really? Because I can reflect back to being a player with, and manager of some of the finest players that have ever been in the game."

"The public can't be kidded. They know what they want to see, what is good and what is bad and what is just average. At least I believe they do."

"We must always consider our supporters, for without them there would be no professional football. It would be better to have more fans watching football the way they like it played, rather than have a few fans watching football the way we would like it played."

"It's no use just winning, we've got to win well."

"There's no use being satisfied when things are done wrongly. I want perfection."

"It is better to fail aiming high than to succeed aiming low. And we of Spurs have set our sights very high, so high in fact that even failure will have in it an echo of glory."

"It's been my life, Tottenham Hotspur, and I love the club."

— GREAT SCOTS —

Scotland has provided Spurs with numerous great players and figures down the years, many of whom have been central to the club's history and success. These include:

John Cameron: Player-manager who led the club to its first major honour outside of the Southern League with the 1901 FA Cup.

Peter McWilliam: In his first spell as manager (1912–27) he secured the 1921 FA Cup, returning for a second stint from 1938 to 1942.

Bill Brown: Bucking the trend for hapless Scottish goalkeepers, Brown was dependable and brave, and a key component of Bill Nicholson's first great side.

Dave Mackay: "He would storm into things with his bloody chest out and that Scottish brawn," said Bill Nicholson of the rock on which the Double team was built. The 'hard man' reputation he resented being labelled with ignored one pertinent point: he was never sent off in his entire career.

John White: The dashing foil for Mackay's armour-plated drive. White's untimely death in 1964 at the age of 26 (he was killed by lightning while out on a golf course) robbed a young family of their husband and father, and Spurs and football of one its most mercurial talents.

Alan Gilzean: A supreme talent as a finisher complemented 'Gilly's' roguish appeal to the fans.

Alfie Conn: With big hair and even bigger sideburns, Conn was the rebellious poster boy for a Spurs support starved of success during the mid-70s wilderness years, but featured in only 49 games. Bill Nick's last signing, he joined from Rangers before a swift return north of the border to Celtic. Asked in a 1985 TV interview which of the Glasgow giants he preferred, Conn replied "Spurs".

Steve Archibald: A single-minded presence in a team of artists, Archibald formed a lethal partnership with Garth Crooks in the trophy-winning side of the early 1980s.

Richard Gough: Viewed by many as the best centre half at the Lane since Mike England, Gough was seen as the final piece in David Pleat's title-tilting side of 1987, but left after only one season for Rangers, citing his wife's homesickness.

— THE WAG CLUB —

Charlotte Mears, Jermain Defoe's dearly beloved and star of ITV's *WAGs Boutique,* used to manage a clothes shop, now works as a model, drives a Range Rover and owns 60 pairs of shoes. She is also a trained boxer.

— IN THE DUG-OUT —

Prior to 1898, various responsibilities were shared between prominent players and officials, but when the club became a limited company in that year, Frank Brettell assumed the more defined role of secretary-manager. Since then, excluding caretakers, Spurs have had 28 managers.

The club's longest-serving manager is Peter McWilliam (19 years over two spells) with Bill Nicholson in the role the most consecutive years (16). David Pleat joins McWilliam in being manager twice, along with Peter Shreeves. The manager for the shortest period was Jacques Santini who lasted barely six months.

Before 1984, the club had 15 managers in 86 years, equating to one managerial change every 5.7 years. Post-1984, there have been 13 managers in 23 years, or a change every 1.7 years. Pre-1984, 14 trophies were lifted, equating to a trophy every 6.1 years; post-1984, the figure is one trophy every 11 years.

Year Appointed	Manager	Honours
1898	Frank Brettell	
1899	John Cameron	FA Cup (1901)
1907	Fred Kirkham	
1912	Peter McWilliam	FA Cup (1921)
1927	Billy Minter	
1930	Percy Smith	
1935	Jack Tresadern	
1938	Peter McWilliam	
1942	Arthur Turner	
1946	Joe Hulme	
1949	Arthur Rowe	League (1951)
1955	Jimmy Anderson	
1958	Bill Nicholson	League (1961), FA Cup (1961,1962, 1967), ECWC (1963), UEFA Cup (1972), League Cup (1971, 1973)
1974	Terry Neill	
1976	Keith Burkinshaw	FA Cup (1981, 1982) UEFA Cup (1984)
1984	Peter Shreeves	
1986	David Pleat	

1987	Terry Venables	FA Cup (1991)
1991	Peter Shreeves	
1992	Doug Livermore & Ray Clemence	
1993	Ossie Ardiles	
1994	Gerry Francis	
1997	Christian Gross	
1998	George Graham	League Cup (1999)
2001	Glenn Hoddle	
2003	David Pleat	
2004	Jacques Santini	
2004	Martin Jol	

— THE YEAR OF THE COCK-A-DOODLE-DO —

The cockerel, or rooster, is one of the 12 signs in the Chinese zodiac. Since the club's formation in 1882, there have been 11 instances when the 'Year of the Rooster' has occurred. Those hoping for good omens for 2017 might want to consider the following:

1885: A legend is born. In the first three years of its existence, the club is known simply as 'Hotspur'. To avoid confusion with another side called London Hotspur (long defunct), founder member Sam Casey amends the name to 'Tottenham Hotspur'. The highlight of the season is when the club meet the famous Casuals in the London Cup. Tottenham Hotspur are beaten 8–0.

1897: Tottenham's debut season in the Southern League ends with a very respectable fourth place. They also compete in the United League, finishing eighth.

1909: After years of success as one of London's pre-eminent clubs (Spurs had been dubbed 'the flower of the south'), Tottenham are finally allowed to join the Football League, securing promotion to the top flight by goal difference at the first attempt.

1921: Spurs win the FA Cup for the second time in their history, beating Wolves 1–0 at a rain-sodden Stamford Bridge, thanks to a Jimmy Dimmock goal.

1933: After a five-year sabbatical in the Second Division, Spurs regain their top-flight status.

1945: World War II ends and Spurs are champions of the Football League South for the second year in succession, losing only one of their 30 matches, albeit in a temporary, breakaway league that bore no competitive relation to peacetime football.

1957: Spurs finish as runners-up to League champions Manchester United by eight points, but outscore Busby's Babes, notching 104 in the league alone.

1969: An underwhelming season of undone promise. Spurs finish sixth in the league and exit the FA Cup at the sixth round stage. On December 17th 1969, the home game against Everton is abandoned after 29 minutes due to floodlight failure.

1981: Another Year of the Cockerel, another FA Cup win, this time in arguably the competition's best-ever final. Ricky Villa struts confidently cockerel-like past the Manchester City defenders, who panic like flustered chickens in a hencoop, to score Wembley's greatest-ever goal. A real-live cockerel, smuggled in by fans, made an appearance on the Hillsborough turf in the preceding semi-final against Wolves.

1993: Spurs meet Arsenal for the second FA Cup semi-final between the old rivals in two years, but this time are robbed. Denied a penalty after a blatant foul on Darren Anderton, Tottenham eventually lose 1–0, thanks to a goal scored by Tony Adams. Spookily, Adams was born in 1966 in the Year of the Horse, an animal that is uncannily similar to a donkey.

2005: With Martin Jol appointed as head coach in the wake of Jacques Santini's unlamented departure, he becomes the fourth man to pick the first team in just two years – an illustration of Tottenham's perennial status as a club 'in transition'. The team finish a disappointing ninth, but this is a significant improvement on the 14th place of the previous campaign. In the summer, Dutch legend Edgar Davids signs for the club.

— SLAM DUNKIN' SPURS —

Canadian basketball legend Steve Nash, guard for the Phoenix Suns, is a die-hard Spurs fan thanks to the influence of his British dad. And judging by comments he made in the middle of the 2006/07 season, he'd like to take that support a stage further.

"If someone were to come in to buy Spurs, I would like to be involved and partner them," said Steve. "Obviously, it would have to make sense for all parties, but, as a fan, it appears to me that Spurs are quite profitable and Premiership football teams are obviously becoming a popular investment for businessmen from all over the world."

— WHO ATE ALL THE MUTTON? —

The attendance of 114,815 at the 1901 FA Cup final between Spurs and Sheffield United was a world record for a football game at the time. To feed the vast crowd, caterers at Crystal Palace laid on:

12,000 slices of bread and butter
4,500 loaves
21,000 rolls
55,120 portions of cake
1,000 sponge cakes
1,000 pieces of shortbread
20,000 French pastries
10,000 Bath buns
10,000 plain buns
24,000 scones
6,000 pork pies
2,000 smoked sausages
1,728 gallons of milk
200 rumps of beef
250 chines of mutton
150 best ends of mutton
60 foreribs of beef
40 whole lambs
300 quarters of whitebait
500lb soles
22,400lb potatoes
2,000 cabbages and cauliflowers
400 fowls
200 ducks
120,000 bottles of mineral water

Not only was there an enormous array of food on offer, there are no reports of anything running out at half-time!

— FROG CHORUS —

For some years up until the mid-1980s, fans standing in the section of terracing below the Shelf in the north-east corner of the ground didn't feel comfortable until they heard the call of The Bullfrog – a loud burp that reverberated around the terrace from a fellow fan at the back of The Shelf who evidently relished the beer and pies provided by club catering.

— FABLE OF THE GABLE —

Roosting proudly atop the old West Stand for 48 years was the original cockerel and ball statue that helped define White Hart Lane's unique character. This was made by former amateur player and craftsman WJ Scott and placed on the stand in 1910, and was transferred to the East Stand in 1958.

Legend had it that a secret Spurs-related treasure had been placed into the ball as a time capsule, but when the old statue was taken down to be replaced by a fibreglass replacement in 1989 all that was found was a rain soaked and tatty club yearbook from 1909.

White Hart Lane's famous cockerel statue

— WHITE NOISE —

How's this for a supergroup of Tottenham-supporting musicians and performers?

Guitar, lead vocals – Bob Marley
Guitar – Jeff Beck
Drums – Dave Clark
Bass –Bruce Foxton (The Jam)
Sax – Steve Norman (Spandau Ballet)
Backing vocals – Shaznay Lewis, Shania Twain, Emma Bunton, Lemar
Turntables – Norman Jay
Roadies – Status Quo
Manager – Jim Callaghan (Rolling Stones)
Support band – Lush

— BRIEFS ENCOUNTER —

Among Tottenham's 2007 UEFA Cup opponents were FC Braga. The meeting was given added spice by the fact that supporters of the Portuguese side dub themselves the 'Arsenalistas'. The association with Tottenham's implacable foe dates back to the 1930s when Braga coach Jose Szabo returned from seeing Arsenal at Highbury and convinced the club to change their colours from green to red with white sleeves. The Braga youth team is even called Arsenal de Braga.

Spurs fans may care to note that the word 'braga', when translated into Spanish, means 'knickers'.

Other Braga Briefs:

- Spurs and Braga met in the first round of the 1984/85 UEFA Cup, with the Londoners emerging triumphant. Winning 3–0 in Portugal, they then stuffed the Arsenalistas 6–0 at White Hart Lane with Garth Crooks bagging a hat trick.
- Spurs defender Riccardo 'Ferrero' Rocha was born in Braga and spent several seasons at the club.

— THE FIRST FOREIGNER —

Osvaldo Ardiles and Ricardo Villa are credited with sparking the influx of foreign players into the English game in the modern era, but the first foreigner to appear in the English football league was another, lesser-known, Spurs star.

German striker Max Seeburg joined the club in May 1907 and made several appearances in the Southern League, before making history by turning out for Spurs the next season in Division Two of the Football League away at Hull on September 26th 1908. Spurs lost 1–0, and Seeburg never made the first team again.

Seeburg, who had played for Cheshunt before turning professional, also played for Chelsea, Leyton Orient, Burnley, Grimsby and Reading. Strictly speaking, he wasn't foreign, as he had moved to London from Leipzig in 1886 at the age of two when his father set up a fur shop. But the authorities considered him a German national, and interned him for several weeks at the start of the First World War.

He eventually settled in Reading, where he died in 1972.

— WHITE HART LANE 1: THE WEST STAND —

White Hart Lane has evolved over a century from a classic late-Victorian football ground into a modern sporting arena. Even within the high-tech design of today's almost uniform bowl, each side of the stadium maintains its own distinct character.

The West Stand has traditionally been the 'blue riband' area of the ground and long the home of more well-to-do supporters. Set away from the High Road and approached via a cul-de-sac now named Bill Nicholson Way, the first West Stand was a rather temporary wooden structure, brought over from the club's previous ground at Northumberland Park. Its successor was an altogether grander design, created by 'football's architect' Archibald Leitch and opened on September 11th 1909.

From the off, it was the seat of power at White Hart Lane, accommodating 6,000 fans in a concrete terraced paddock at the front and 5,300 seated spectators in the top wooden-floored tier, with the directors' box and press box positioned above the halfway line. The dressing rooms were sited underneath, with the players emerging up a short tunnel, and by the early 1960s, below a blue and white sign of a cockerel. Outside, above a sweep of steps, the back of the building was a broad flank of non-descript corrugated iron, but it bore the legend 'Tottenham Hotspur Football Club' in huge white letters.

The West Stand gabled roof provided the original roost for the cockerel-and-ball statue (See *Fable of the Gable*, page 46). The stand also provided the backdrop to many of Tottenham's greatest moments, including the presentation of the League trophy in 1961. The only significant changes were the additions of corner sections that linked up quite awkwardly with the North and South Stands.

By the late 1970s the stand was well past its best. Plans were finalised in 1980 to completely rebuild it, and these were later adapted by a new regime in the boardroom. The bold scheme was for a double-tiered, all-seater stand with a sweeping cantilevered roof removing the need for any pillars that would block supporters' views. Fundamental to the revenue-raising objectives were two tiers of executive boxes that eventually numbered 72 in total. The architects Mather and Nutter described it as a 'hotel with seats on top'. In addition the club offices were sited behind the stand in a smoked-glass block architecturally in tune with 1980s' styles.

Officially opened on February 6th 1982 by Olympic sprint champion Alan Wells and former FIFA President Sir Stanley Rous, the gleaming new construction got off to a good start as Spurs thrashed Wolves 6–1, but behind the scenes the development had cost the club dear. The price of construction had soared to almost £6m, helping to saddle the club with debts of £5m that were only tackled when the club became a plc in 1983.

Just 24 years later, the West Stand is already showing its age. With some matchday seats costing up to £70 and the boxes virtually full, it provides substantial revenue but the capacity, 6,891, is severely limited. Sightlines from the shallow bottom tier are not to everyone's tastes, notably the press corps, whose position to the side of the tunnel and behind the dug-outs have led to many a grumbling hack complaining about the view. Depending on plans for the further development of White Hart Lane, the future of the West Stand is uncertain.

— SANDY IN THE BOX —

During the 1900/01 FA Cup run, forward Alexander 'Sandy' Brown became the first player to score in every round of the cup in one season, notching 15 goals. This total also secured Brown the record for the most goals scored in one FA Cup season.

— MIXED OPPONENTS —

Since Spurs joined the Football League in 1908, they have entertained 75 visiting sides and played at 89 different away grounds. At two grounds they have played two different clubs – Hull City and Leeds United at Boothferry Park, and Queens Park Rangers and Fulham at Loftus Road. At one ground, Selhurst Park, Spurs have played three different clubs – Crystal Palace, Wimbledon and Charlton Athletic. Meanwhile, games against Manchester City have been played at three separate grounds – Hyde Road, Maine Road and the City of Manchester Stadium.

— PERRYMAN'S LORE —

"Wherever Spurs play, whether it's Manchester, Malta or Mauritius, we're famous. Soccer is about big clubs and star names, but most of all it's about people. You can be playing for the biggest club in the world with the biggest stars in the game, but if you don't enjoy it, if you don't get on with the people around you, you're wasting your time.

"I enjoy Spurs because at this club everyone, from the humblest backroom boy to the highest-paid player, is treated with equal respect. They're all equally important to our success. That's what makes Tottenham Hotspur a great football club."

Steve Perryman, writing in the club's centenary programme, 1982.

— LIGHTS, CAMERA AND . . . LILYWHITE ACTION! —

Highlights of Spurs on the silver and small screens.

Those Glory Glory Days (1983)

Adapted from her own semi-autobiographical story by *Times* sports journalist Julie Welch, *Those Glory Glory Days* is an unashamed wallow in sixties nostalgia, celebrating the captivating magic of the Double side as seen through the eyes of the fictional Julia and her teenage friends growing up in London. The action flits between the girls' adoration of the players and a desperate search for cup final tickets, and contemporary scenes in which the now grown up Julia tracks down her heroes to make a documentary.

Danny Blanchflower played himself in the up-to-date sections filmed in the White Hart Lane press box; former Crystal Palace player John Salthouse played the young Danny in the flashbacks.

Life is Sweet (1990)

Mike Leigh's slice of North London life features a typical pub football conversation between two embittered and inebriated Tottenham fans, Andy (Jim Broadbent) and Patsy (Stephen Rea), praising the achievements of the Double side and mocking the boring football of the Arsenal's 1971 double winners.

Bedknobs and Broomsticks (1971)

Disney's blend of live action and cartoon wizardry sensibly acknowledged the box office value of a Spurs reference. Shortly before a football match between two teams of animated animals, Dr Emelius Browne (David Tomlinson) volunteers to be referee, "I used to play for Tottenham Hotspur, you know." Spurs fan Bruce Forsyth played the role of nasty spiv Swinburne.

The Invisible Man (1933)

Actress Merle Tottenham played Millie in the original version of the horror film classic. Claims that the title refers to Jaques Santini's 'now you see him, now you don't' tenure at White Hart Lane are entirely without substance.

Kes (1969)

"We'll be Man United, you can be Spurs'" says the brilliant Brian Glover, playing the ludicrous bullying PE teacher Mr Sugden, as he kicks off a game of school football at a Barnsley comprehensive. Director Ken Loach, a keen football fan, ensured 'Spurs' came out on top, beating Sugden's 'Man U' 2–1.

Porridge (1974–77)
British television's greatest sitcom centred around crafty old lag Norman Stanley Fletcher and his never-ending quest to earn 'little victories' over the prison establishment. Tottenham-supporting Fletch got a major result in the classic episode 'Men Without Women', conning the prison governor into awarding him compassionate leave on trumped up marital grounds. After his weekend back home in Muswell Hill, Fletcher returned to Slade prison to gloat over his fellow inmates: "Some of us have been in the pub or eating roast beef or watching Spurs win at home. Or having a sing-song with their friends and relatives. Or lying in their big, crisp bed, with their big, crisp old lady."

2.4 Children (1991–1999)
A mediocre BBC sitcom, redeemed by casting the father and son as Tottenham supporters. Dad was played by the late Gary Olsen, a Spurs fan in real life

Notes on a Scandal (2006)
The acclaimed film version of Zoe Heller's novel centres on a tempestuous love triangle in an inner-city London school. But the highlight for Tottenham supporters comes in a scene when a friend of Dame Judi Dench's character informs her he's just spent a gleeful afternoon at White Hart Lane watching a Spurs win inspired by Jermain Defoe. Dench mournfully comments on her father's lifelong support of Charlton Athletic, and how "it had brought him so very little pleasure".

— SINKING THE KOP —

When Spurs beat Liverpool 2–1 at Anfield on March 16th 1912, the team could not know it would be 73 years to the day before they beat The Reds on their own turf again.

The Anfield hoodoo became a bigger story every year, with the press taking great delight in pointing out that Spurs had not won at Anfield since the Titanic went down.

So as the jubilant team of 1985 travelled home after Garth Crooks had netted the goal in a historic 1–0 win, defender Paul Miller said loudly: "I bet the passengers of the QE2 are s**tting themselves tonight!"

— SPURS WORLD OF SPORT —

Sports stars who are Spurs fans:

Dennis Bergkamp
John Gregory
Steve Nash (NBA basketball player)
Peter Forsberg (ice hockey player)
Ian Thorpe (swimmer)
Mike Gatting
Darren Gough
Chris Eubank
Barry McGuigan
Roy Gumbs (boxer)
Ronnie O'Sullivan (well, before he defected to Arsenal)
Peter Ebdon (snooker player)
Russell Claydon (golfer)
Mark Foster (swimmer)
Tim Foster (rower)
Ken Tyrell (deceased motor racing legend)
Richie Benaud
Mark Alleyne (cricketer)
Wayne 'Hawaii 501' Mardle (darts player)

— 'AND THEY CALL IT TOTTENHAM LOVE' —

As the teen idol of his day, Donny Osmond would have been a conspicuous attendee at the White Hart Lane game against Leicester in April 1974, had he not slipped through the turnstiles incognito. Such was the singer's enormous popularity at the time, there were genuine security concerns, so Osmond turned up in disguise – dressed as a tramp, of all things – to see Spurs beat the Foxes 1–0, thanks to a Martin Chivers goal.

"Everyone in North America has their favourite soccer team and mine is Spurs," warbled Donny.

— THE PAYNE'S BOOTS AFFAIR —

Over the years, the football authorities have not always been kind to Tottenham Hotspur. But an early injustice brought positive results for the club, after an incident that became notorious as the 'Payne's Boots Affair'.

Ernie Payne was a left-winger with Fulham who had yet to play for the west Londoners' first team. At the beginning of the 1893/94 season Spurs offered him a game. As both clubs were amateur, Payne could move where he wanted, and deals of this sort were common practice. On the morning of his debut, for a game against Old St Marks in the first round of the London Senior Cup, Payne found he had no kit. Spurs didn't have a pair of boots in his size, so gave him 10 shillings to buy a pair on the understanding that the boots would belong to the club.

Fulham complained about this to the London FA, accusing Spurs of poaching and unfair inducement. Spurs were found guilty and suspended from the league for a fortnight, while Payne was suspended for a week. The extraordinary decision generated much publicity and huge sympathy for Spurs, and the team began to draw large crowds wherever they played. The affair also brought the club to the attention of wealthy businessman John Oliver, who became president and began to put Spurs on the map, bringing in a professional trainer and building a stand at the Northumberland Park ground. The London FA's ruling also convinced the club that it should go professional.

— BROTHER BEYOND —

At home against Bradford City on January 29th 1910, Spurs fielded three brothers in the first team for the first and only time. Bob and Danny Steel had long careers with the club between 1908 and 1912, racking up 314 and 165 appearances respectively. For this game they were joined by younger brother Alexander, although this was to be his one and only appearance in club colours.

— HOME SWEET HOME —

Tottenham legend Steve Perryman on the difference between Spurs and Arsenal, in his autobiography *A Man for All Seasons*: "Highbury has always seemed a very cold, unappealing place to me . . . inside [Spurs], the people are warm and it has always seemed a much friendlier club than Arsenal, with a lot more life about it."

— FIRST LEAGUE GAME —

Tottenham Hotspur's first game in the Football League was a Division Two fixture at home to then FA Cup holders Wolverhampton Wanderers on September 1st 1908, the opening day of the 1908/09 season,

Spurs had been unhappy with the Southern League since the 'Payne's Boots Affair' (See The *Payne's Boots Affair*, page 53) and when Stoke City resigned from the Football League, they applied for the vacant place. Lincoln City also put in an application, and the vote was a close thing. In the first ballot, Rotherham Town and Southport didn't secure a single vote. Stoke City, who had changed their mind and re-applied, registered six, and Spurs and Lincoln tied on 17. In the run-off, Spurs and Lincoln each secured 20 votes, so it was left to the League's management committee to vote 5–3 in favour of the London club. It's thought the lustre of the 1901 FA Cup win swung the vote for Spurs.

A crowd of 20,000 turned out to see that first game and were delighted when Vivian Woodward scored for Spurs after just six minutes. Woodward bagged another at the start of the second half and Tom Morris scored the third in a 3–0 win for the home side. Spurs had entered the League in style, and went on to gain promotion to the top flight at the end of that first season.

The first ever Spurs team in the league was:

Hewitson, Coquet, Burton, Morris, D Steel, Darnell, Walton, Woodward, McFarlane, R Steel, Middlemiss.

— SPURS PLAYERS OF THE YEAR —

[Note: the PFA Player of the Year (PFA) awards began in 1974, the Football Writer's Association (FWA) in 1948.]

Year	Player	Award
1958	Danny Blanchflower	FWA
1961	Danny Blanchflower	FWA
1973	Pat Jennings	FWA
1976	Pat Jennings	PFA
1980	Glenn Hoddle	PFA Young Player of the Year
1982	Steve Perryman	FWA
1987	Clive Allen	PFA & FWA
1992	Gary Lineker	FWA
1995	Jurgen Klinsmann	FWA
1999	David Ginola	PFA & FWA

— PRACTICE MAKES PERFECT —

"Waterloo was won on the playing fields of Eton," the Duke of Wellington was said to have claimed – but what about winning football trophies? Here's where Tottenham's training ground routines have been honed down the years.

Tottenham Marshes. Drainage was a problem, but the wide-open (if windblown) spaces besides the River Lea to the east of the High Road provided a cheap and cheerful venue for early training.

The White Hart Lane indoor ball court. Tucked behind the West Stand, this rudimentary gymnasium was short on facilities but ideal for developing the fast-passing, spirited style of the great post-war sides. When Dave Mackay arrived the level of competitiveness went up another notch; trainer Cecil Poynton used to lock the door and let the players get on with it. Now used as a matchday car park.

Cheshunt, Brookfield Lane. The site of Cheshunt FC's former ground up the A10 featured an impressive array of full size pitches, set in a leafy Hertfordshire suburb close to the homes of many players. Sold for £5m in the 1980s and redeveloped into a housing estate.

Spurs Lodge, Chigwell. Opened by Tony Blair on September 21st 1996, the Lodge has provided Spurs with a permanent modern training centre after the rudimentary public park facilities of Mill Hill.

— SHEER POETRY —

Dubbed the 'Flower of the South', at the start of the 20th century Tottenham were gaining increasing support amongst the general public of north London, as illustrated in 1900 by the publication of the following verse in the *Tottenham Herald*. Note the use of 'Hotspurs', as the club was then popularly referred to as.

What care I of things South African
Or whether the Boers will fight,
Or that France has ceased to know the way,
Between what is wrong and right?
I care not for things political,
Or which party's out or in,
The only thing I trouble about,
Is will Tottenham Hotspurs win?

— WALTER TULL —

His life story reads like the stuff of *Boys Own* fiction but Walter Tull's heroism and determination to overcome the odds from childhood serve as a reminder that football really isn't more important than life and death. Tull was Tottenham's first black footballer and English football's first black outfield player (following in the footsteps of Preston North End goalkeeper Arthur Wharton) – achievements in their own right, but it is his subsequent military career that brings Tull's fame into sharp relief.

Born in Folkestone in 1888 to a Barbadian father who had married a local woman, he had lost both his parents by the age of nine and with his brother Edward was sent to an orphanage in Bethnal Green. Excelling at athletics and football, Walter played for Clapton FC, winning medals and the title of the *Football Star* periodical's 'catch of the season'.

In 1909, Spurs snapped him up and he was soon impressing with his speed and skill as an inside-left. However, in a match at Bristol City, he was subjected to racist insults from the home crowd. The *Football Star*'s reporter wrote: 'A section of the spectators made a cowardly attack on him in language lower than Billingsgate. Let me tell those Bristol hooligans that Tull is so clean in mind and method as to be a model for all white men who play football whether they be amateur or professional. In point of ability, if not actual achievement, Tull was the best forward on the field.'

Sadly, Tottenham did not display the same determination that Tull had, and after just three more appearances, he was sold. Perhaps the club feared the abuse might escalate into something more physical, compromising the safety of Tull and other players; more likely the club's decision reflected the climate of the time when standing up for a mixed-race player was a low priority.

Moving on to Northampton Town (there is a memorial garden dedicated to Tull at the club's Sixfields Stadium) he made 110 appearances and scored nine goals, and was on the verge of joining Glasgow Rangers when the First World War broke out.

He signed up straight away to join the 17th (1st Football) Battalion of the Middlesex Regiment, arriving in France in 1915, where his leadership qualities soon earned him promotion to the rank of sergeant. He fought in the First Battle of the Somme in 1916, but was sent home after catching trench fever. Nonetheless, he had impressed his commanding officers to such an extent that he was recommended for a commission, despite the then official colour bar that prevented 'any negro or person of colour' rising above the rank

SPURS
Home Kits
1881-2008

www.historicalkits.co.uk

1882-84 (Hotspur)

1884-86

1890-96

1896-98

1898-1903

1903-09

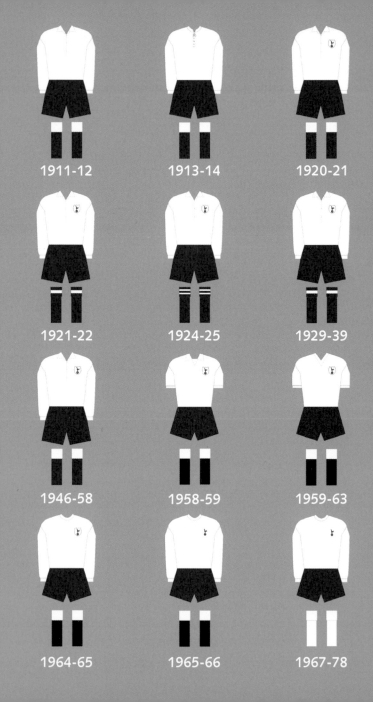

1911-12

1913-14

1920-21

1921-22

1924-25

1929-39

1946-58

1958-59

1959-63

1964-65

1965-66

1967-78

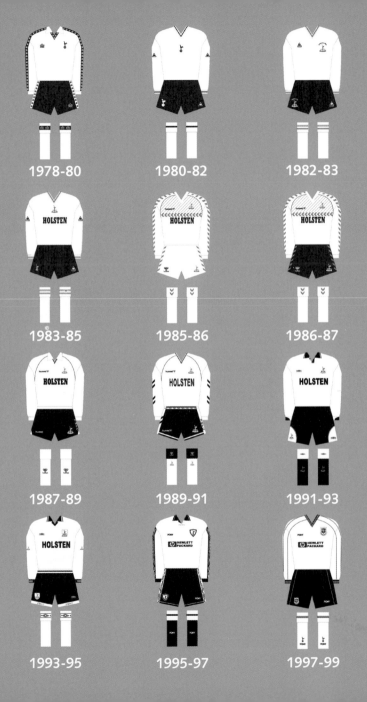

1978-80

1980-82

1982-83

1983-85

1985-86

1986-87

1987-89

1989-91

1991-93

1993-95

1995-97

1997-99

1999-2001

2001-02

2002-04

2004-05

2005-06

2006-07

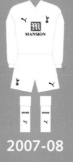
2007-08

of NCO. He thus became the first-ever black officer in the British Army.

Returning to the front line, Lieutenant Tull was mentioned in dispatches for his coolness and gallantry under fire in Italy, before switching back to the Western front. One day in the closing months of the conflict, Tull was ordered to lead an assault on German positions and was brought down in No Man's Land. It speaks volumes for his popularity as a leader and comrade that his men made repeated, courageous attempts to rescue him but he succumbed to his wounds before he could be brought back to British lines. His body was never found. Awarded the British War medal and recommended for the MC, Tull died on the March 25th 1918.

Walter Tull: a true 'Boys Own Hero'

— SEMI-DETACHED SPURS —

Popular football wisdom has it that it's far worse to lose a semi-final than a final itself. Well, Tottenham have triumphed in 19 out of 35 semis in all competitions, with Spurs managers having to trot out the standard 'now we can concentrate on the league' line on 16 occasions.

Here is a full run down of Tottenham's semi-final appearances, by competition:

FA CUP
Semi-finals: 17

1901 Spurs 4, West Brom 0 (won in final)
1921 Spurs 2, Preston NE 1 (won in final)
1922 Spurs 1, Preston NE 2
1948 Spurs 1, Blackpool 3
1953 Spurs 1, Blackpool 2
1956 Spurs 0, Man City 1
1961 Spurs 3, Burnley 0 (won in final)
1962 Spurs 3, Man U 1 (won in final)
1967 Spurs 2, Notts Forest 1 (won in final)
1981 Spurs 3, Wolves 0 (replay; won in final)
1982 Spurs 2, Leicester 0 (won in final)
1987 Spurs 4, Watford 1 (lost in final)
1991 Spurs 3, Arsenal 1 (St Hotspur's Day; won in final)
1993 Spurs 0, Arsenal 1
1995 Spurs 1, Everton 4
1999 Spurs 0, Newcastle 2
2001 Spurs 1, Arsenal 2

LEAGUE CUP
Semi-finals: 11
(Scores are aggregate results unless otherwise stated)

1968 Spurs 1, Arsenal 2
1971 Spurs 3, Bristol City 1 (aet; won in final)
1972 Spurs 4, Chelsea 5
1973 Spurs 4, Wolves 3 (won in final)
1976 Spurs 2, Newcastle 3
1982 Spurs 1, West Brom 0 (lost in final)
1987 Spurs 1, Arsenal 2 (replay)
1992 Spurs 2, Notts Forest 3
1999 Spurs 1, Wimbledon 0 (won in final)
2002 Spurs 6, Chelsea 3 (lost in final)
2007 Spurs 3, Arsenal 5

EUROPE
Semi-finals: 7

1962 EC Spurs 3, Benfica 4
1963 ECWC Spurs 5, OFK Belgrade 2 (agg; won in final)
1972 UEFA Spurs 3, AC Milan 2 (agg; won in final)
1973 UEFA Spurs 2, Liverpool 2 (agg; lost on away goals)
1974 UEFA Spurs 4, Lokomotiv Leipzig 1(agg; lost final)
1982 ECWC Spurs 1, Barcelona 2 (agg)
1984 UEFA Spurs 2 Hajduk Split 2 (agg; won on away goals, won final)

— THE PHILOSOPHICAL DIVIDE —

"If Ossie Ardiles had gone to Arsenal, they would have had him marking the opposing goalkeeper, or something."
Danny Blanchflower

"Steve Perryman, he's never a Spurs player, he's too good a defender. He should have been at Arsenal."
George Male, former England and Arsenal captain and chief scout.

— ANY PUBLICITY IS GOOD PUBLICITY —

There were red faces all round at Spurs after the 1987 FA Cup final – not just because Tottenham had lost 3–2 to Coventry, but because a pre-match mix up meant half the team took to the pitch wearing new shirts sporting the logo of sponsors Holsten while the rest (among them Glenn Hoddle) wore plain shirts. A kit faux pas it may have been but it gained Holsten huge publicity in the next day's papers.

— THINK PINK —

For the opening away leg against Unizale Textile Arad, in the UEFA Cup quarter-final on March 7th 1972, Tottenham's Romanian opponents wore pink shirts for the first half – and inexplicably switched to red for the second.

— CLASSIC MATCHES 3: A BUNCH OF FIVES —

Spurs 5	**Aston Villa 5**
Gilzean,	Hateley (4),
Greaves,	Deakin
Saul,	
Brown,	
Robertson	

March 19th 1966: Division One
White Hart Lane
Att: 28,290

In recent years, Spurs have developed a bit of a reputation for losing games they were comfortably ahead in. But none of them matched the drama of this game in which Spurs were 5–1 up but could have lost 6–5 if it wasn't for a late goal-line clearance by Alan Mullery.

The game was a personal disaster for Tottenham's Laurie Brown, as Spurs fan Chris Kaufman remembers well. Now a national official for the Transport and General Workers Union, Chris had been talked into taking a delegation of Russian trade unionists to the match due to the fact that he could speak a little Russian. He tells the story in *We Are Tottenham*, (Cloake and Powley, Mainstream 2004):

It was in the days when Spurs had this Laurie Brown. They got him off the Arsenal, which always proves to be a bad move. It was all Spurs attacking and by half time they were 5–1 up. Then Aston Villa got it back to 5–2, and then I noticed that every time Laurie Brown went anywhere near the ball the whole Spurs defence fell into a kind of collective St Vitus Dance cum nervous breakdown.

It went to 5–4, the ball bounced off Laurie Brown's ankle straight into the path of one of their forwards. So I got up and I said, 'Look, this is how we do it in England, we should go,' because I knew what would happen, being a Spurs supporter.

And lo, that is what happened. I think Laurie Brown got the ball and he just had to pass it out and he gave it to some Villa player, there was a little exchange of passes and the ball ended up in the Spurs net. By that time there was no point in me saying go or not go. It was excruciating for me, but the Russians thought it was wonderful. But that's what being a Spurs supporter is about.

— SPURS LEGENDS: CHRIS WADDLE —

Chris Waddle: two haircuts in one!

He worked in sausage factory, recorded a top 20 duet and blazed a trail for one of the worst haircuts in sporting history – but in between such varying achievements, Chris Waddle was a wonderful footballer. Christopher Roland Waddle began his career playing for local sides in the Gateshead area, and after the aforementioned spell making bangers and meat pies, signed for Newcastle. A right-winger in the classic mould, Waddle impressed Spurs boss Peter Shreeves and was brought to White Hart Lane in 1985 for a fee of £590,000. He took a while to settle, but once established in a squad that still boasted the midfield talents of Glenn Hoddle and Ossie Ardiles, Waddle became an incisive creative force in a team committed to attack. Paired with Clive Allen on the pitch, Waddle was devastating in the 1986/87 season, helping the striker to plunder an incredible 49 goals. Off the pitch he teamed up with Hoddle to record 'Diamond Lights' and appear on *Top of the Pops*, by then having ditched the 'two-haircuts-in-one' mullet for a more sober style.

Despite such successes, however, Waddle was destined to become the nearly man in a nearly team. Spurs lost out in the league Cup semi final to Arsenal, lost the FA Cup Final to Coventry and finished third in the league as a backlog of games tripped up their title challenge.

After 138 appearances and 33 goals, Waddle was sold for what new manager Terry Venables called £4.5m of 'silly money' to Olympic Marseille, Tottenham's willingness to take the cash an early indicator of the financial problems that were to plague the club two years later.

Now a popular summariser and pundit for the BBC, Waddle maintains an undying faith in the principles of fluent, entertaining football that characterised his spell at Spurs. In essence he is the inheritor of Danny Blanchflower's philosophy, once saying: "All fans want to see their teams win, but they love it even more when they're entertained as well. I like the thought of someone leaving the ground and going into work or the schoolyard on Monday morning and saying 'Hey, you should have seen what Waddle did to this full-back'. People always remember Johan Cruyff's back-heel flick far more than any goal he ever scored. That's what football's about. Giving people something to smile about."

— THE FIRST DERBY —

The first Tottenham v Arsenal game was played on November 19th 1887 on Tottenham Marshes. Royal Arsenal, as the Gunners were then called, had yet to move to north London, but they exhibited some traits that would become familiar over the years.

After arriving late, Arsenal scored an early goal and proceeded to defend for the rest of the game, indicating an early preference for the '1–0 to the Arsenal' approach that would become infamous a century later. This proved a mistake as, with 15 minutes to go, Spurs led 2–1. At this point the Arsenal players began to complain of 'lack of light' and the match was called off.

The seeds of a long rivalry were sown, as possibly was the tradition of those connected with Arsenal claiming they 'did not see' at convenient times.

— ARDILES HITS THE ROOF —

Ever wondered why, in any pictures taken of the FA Cup after Spurs won it in the famous 1981 final, a hand can be seen over the rim of the trophy?

As the players celebrated in the dressing room after the replay, Ossie Ardiles was happier than most. Fuelled by adrenalin and a few glasses of champagne, the little midfielder grabbed the Cup and leapt into the huge, deep bath. As he did so he threw the Cup in the air, and it crashed against the ceiling, denting the rim.

In all subsequent photographs the damage is craftily concealed, and the club made sure the dent was repaired before returning the trophy to the FA.

— WORLD CLASS —

The four World Cup winners who have played for Spurs are:

Martin Peters, England 1966

Described by Ron Greenwood, his then manager at West Ham, as being 'ten years ahead of his time', Peters switched from East London to join Spurs in March 1970 for a record £200,000 (with Jimmy Greaves heading the other way in part-exchange). Peters played 260 times for Tottenham, scoring 76 goals.

The all-round talents as a midfielder that gave rise to Greenwood's tribute found their natural home at White Hart Lane, and Peters won a UEFA Cup and two League Cup winners medals before transferring to Norwich City in February 1975 for £40,000 as part of manager Terry Neill's clear out. Neill was proved to have discarded the World Cup winner prematurely as Peters went on to play a further 232 times for Norwich, scoring 50 goals.

In total, Peters played 67 times for his country (four as captain), scoring 20 goals, the most famous being the 'other' goal in the World Cup victory of 1966. In 1998, after a successful business career, Peters returned to Tottenham to join the board as a non-executive director.

Osvaldo Ardiles, Argentina 1978

At just 5ft 6ins and with a fighting weight of only 9 stone 10lbs, Ossie Ardiles might have looked more like the lawyer he trained to become rather than the outstanding professional footballer he was, but in two spells with Spurs he became one of the club's genuine legends. Ardiles was the midfield fulcrum of Cesar Menotti's World-Cup winning side and emerged as one of the first and most successful of all foreign imports into the British game.

Ardiles played 293 times for Spurs, scoring 25 goals during two spells at White Hart Lane, between 1978–1982 and 1983–1988, with the intervening period on loan at Paris St Germain due to the Falklands War (Ardiles' cousin, Flight Lieutenant José Ardiles, a pilot in the Argentinian air force, was killed in the conflict).

Former Liverpool defender Tommy Smith was one of those traditional English hard men who salivated at the prospect of physically intimidating the diminutive Ardiles, saying "he can't expect not to be tackled just because Argentina won the World Cup." Soon, however, opponents came to realise they were dealing with a genuine world-class player, and that trying to dispossess Ardiles was, as former Everton hero Joe Royle said, "like tackling dust".

Ardiles' football philosophy was perfectly attuned to Tottenham's 'glory glory' credo: "I'll never compromise my ideals, whichever division I'm in," he said on becoming manager at Swindon. "I tell the boys to play like Pele." Not the sort of instruction, you imagine, that can have been heard that often at the County Ground.

As well as being an inspirational manager, Ossie wasn't averse to a spot of self-promotion either. Asked if he thought Jürgen Klinsmann was Tottenham's biggest ever signing, Ardiles replied wryly, "No, I was." Many Spurs fans would wholeheartedly agree.

Ricardo Villa, Argentina 1978

Ricky Villa did not last as long as his compatriot at White Hart Lane, leaving in 1983 after 168 games and 25 goals; nor did he enjoy such universal admiration.

Prior to his arrival in July 1978 after two substitute appearances in the World Cup tournament, one commentator highlighted a Villa foul, remarking that this was not the kind of behaviour "people want to see in the English game". Such a short-sighted attitude overlooked Villa's skill, power and sureness of touch and with his winning goal in the 1981 FA Cup final, he made an indelible mark on English football's heritage.

"I'm always overwhelmed by the reaction of the people when I go back to England – I get recognised more here than I do in Argentina," said Villa on the 25th anniversary of the 1981 final. "I get stopped in the street and everyone wants to talk about a goal that I scored so long ago. But I never get fed up with it. It's great that everyone remembers this wonderful moment in the club's history. Wherever I am in England, when people recognise me they always say, 'I've seen your goal – it was fantastic.' And it's not just Spurs fans, it's Manchester United, Liverpool and even Arsenal supporters. That really means a lot to me. It is a great honour to have played such a part in the history of English football."

Jürgen Klinsmann, Germany 1990

As a German, Klinsmann was never going to be the most naturally popular of players with some of the more xenophobic English fans and journalists; as a player with a reputation for diving, that antagonism was even more pronounced. Yet within just a few games of arriving in London, 'Klinsi' had won over even his fiercest critics.

Klinsmann signed for Spurs from AS Monaco on July 29th 1994 for £2m. It was in the principality – specifically aboard chairman Alan Sugar's luxury yacht *Louisiana* – that the deal was struck. The signing had echoes of the transfer coups that brought Ardiles and Villa to north London and reinvigorated a club that had been stumbling around in mid-table mediocrity and rocked by scandal, points deductions and financial penalties off the pitch, stemming from irregular payments in the 1980s. Joined by Romanian international Ilie Dumitrescu and teaming up with Teddy Sheringham, Nicky Barmby and Darren Anderton, Klinsmann became the central figure in then manager Ardiles' 'Famous Five' attack.

In his first game, against Sheffield Wednesday on August 20th 1994, Klinsmann gave a masterful display of the attacking arts, striking up an immediate rapport with Sheringham and prompting team-mates to produce an exciting 4–3 victory, before he was taken off needing 11 stitches in a cut lip. Klinsmann scored the fourth goal with a bullet header and then pulled off a public relations masterstroke by theatrically diving in celebration, mocking his reputation for going down all too easily. Even the Sheffield Wednesday fans applauded.

Despite further upheaval at the club – Ardiles was sacked in November to be replaced by Gerry Francis – Klinsmann scored a fabulous 29 goals that season. Even if his own FA Cup dream was to end in disappointment, with Spurs thrashed 4–1 by Everton in the semi-final, his impact was enormous. He left under something of a cloud, exercising his right to stay just one season and infuriating chairman Alan Sugar who in a TV interview threw Klinsmann's shirt at the reporter, fuming, "I wouldn't wash my car with that." Two years later, however, Klinsi was back on a six-month deal, scoring nine goals in 15 appearances to help rescue Spurs from potential relegation.

— THE 100 CLUB —

To date, 14 players have scored 100 or more goals for Spurs. Leading the list by some margin is Jimmy Greaves with 266 goals, 58 ahead of his 1960s' teammate Bobby Smith.

Only Teddy Sheringham has reached three figures in the last 19 years. This reflects a relative lack of success since the 1960s, but also the fact that players do not tend to stay with the club long enough to reach the 100 mark.

The full list is:

Player	Goals	Appearances	Goal ratio
1. Jimmy Greaves	266	379	70%
2. Bobby Smith	208	317	66%
3. Martin Chivers	174	355	49%
4. Cliff Jones	159	370	43%
5. George Hunt	137	198	69%
6. Len Duquemin	134	307	44%
7. Alan Gilzean	133	429	31%
8. Teddy Sheringham	124	270	46%
9. Les Bennett	118	294	40%
10. Jimmy Dimmock	112	438	26%
11. Glenn Hoddle	110	478	23%
12. Bert Bliss	106	215	49%
13. Jack Morrison	102	154	66%
14. Billy Minter	101	262	39%

— BLUE (AND WHITE) RIBBONED —

One of football's most enduring and symbolic traditions was started by Tottenham. After winning the 1901 FA Cup, Spurs tied ribbons to the trophy in the club colours of blue and white, a practice followed by every victorious side since.

In 1921 when Spurs won the FA Cup again, they used the very same ribbons from the first triumph 20 years before.

— FANCY THAT —

Never mind cockerels, what is it about Spurs and pigeons?

Birds of a Feather: Former manager Gerry Francis is a world-renowned expert on pigeons and an experienced pigeon-fancier, and was even the adviser on the film *Valiant*, which told the heroic tale of carrier pigeons and their service for the armed forces. "The lives they've saved," said Francis, "it's hard to comprehend."

Where Pigeons Dare: In 1988, Paul Gascoigne decided he fancied a spot of shooting practice. Instead of heading out for a clay pigeon shoot in the country, he climbed into the old East Stand press box at White Hart Lane to take a few pot shots at some real pigeons. The press box had been closed for safety reasons, but Gascoigne was undeterred and took up his shooting position – only to fall 15 feet through the rotting floorboards onto the seated tier below. He escaped with minor injuries.

A pigeon

— THE THINGS WE DO FOR LOVE —

Ritual and superstition loom large in the life of any football fan, particularly before derby games. For lifelong Spurs fan Morris Keston, one ritual spanned years.

During the decades in which Keston has followed Tottenham, he's forged friendships with many of the names at the club. One was Terry Venables and, through him, Keston got to know George Graham, then an Arsenal player and a former team-mate of Venables at Chelsea. But after a couple of derby games where Graham had seen Keston in the days leading up to the game and Arsenal had won, the pair both began to believe that Graham seeing Keston before the game was a lucky omen for Arsenal and whenever a derby game approached Keston would go to any lengths to avoid his 'at any other time' pal.

As one derby approached, Keston arrived home on the eve of the game confident of a Spurs victory, as he had managed to avoid Graham in the days before the game. But later that evening his doorbell rang. It was George Graham and, let in by Keston's unsympathetic wife, the Arsenal man began to search the flat until he came to a locked toilet door. Grabbing a chair, he climbed up to peer through the glass window above the door and spotted his mate on the other side.

"I've seen you," he shouted, "now we'll win."

And they did.

— PAYING THE PENALTY —

Spurs have had to go through the mental torture of a penalty shoot-out five times across all competitions, winning two but losing the last three nail-biters. Here's the complete record of Spurs' shoot-out heaven and hell.

Date	Competition	Final score (aet)	Shoot-out score
May 23rd 1984	UEFA Cup final	Spurs 1 Anderlecht 1	Won 4–3
Jan 19th 1994	FA Cup 3rd rnd	Spurs 1 Peterborough 1	Won 5–4
Mar 9th 1996	FA Cup 5th rnd	Spurs 1 Nottm Forest 1	Lost 1–3
Dec17th 2003	League Cup 5th rnd	Spurs 1 Liverpool 1	Lost 5–4
Dec 1st 2004	League Cup 5th rnd	Spurs 1 Middlesbrough	Lost 5–4

— YOU CAN SAY THAT AGAIN —

"I'm no poof, that's for sure."
Paul Gascoigne, on the *Wogan* show

"He loved sex, but he always checked the scores on Teletext first."
Model **Eva Dijkstra**, in her kiss-and-tell revelations about Les
Ferdinand, 1996

"Hoddle a luxury? It's the bad players who are a luxury."
Danny Blanchflower

"In a poor side, Danny [Blanchflower] is an expensive luxury and
that's why I dropped him when we had a poor team. But in a good
side as Spurs are now, he is a wonderful asset through his unorthodox
approach and marvellous ball skill."
Bill Nicholson

Bill Nicholson: "Danny, let me get you a drink, your glass is half
empty."
Danny Blanchflower: "Thank you Bill, but actually, it's half full."
A conversation at a Spurs reception. An exasperated Nicholson was
then heard to mutter "That Blanchflower, I – he's impossible!"

"As far as scoring goals was concerned, Jimmy Greaves was a Picasso."
Clive Allen

"I'm rather a boring sort of person."
Gary Lineker

"Gary Lineker's a bit of a babe."
Boy George

"For a defender, Chris Waddle running at you is the worst sight in
football."
Alan Hansen

"I would run through brick walls for Spurs."
Graham Roberts

"I'm a miserable sod."
Alan Sugar

— THAT SINKING FEELING —

After an impressive 5–2 victory over eventual champions Everton on February 11th 1928, Tottenham's players and supporters would have been forgiven for thinking their team was on the up. As late as April they were healthily placed in mid-table. Less than a month later, however, they finished second from bottom and were relegated to Division Two.

What became known as the freak season ended with the tightest points spread in British football. Seven teams finished with 39 points, just one more than Spurs; fourth-placed Derby ended the campaign with only six more points than Spurs and even Everton only notched 53. Tottenham's tally of 38 points was a relegation record under the old two-points-for-a-win system, but the club were the architects of their own downfall, having allowed striker Jimmy Seed to move to Sheffield Wednesday. Seeds' goals for the Owls saved their top-flight status at Tottenham's expense.

1927/28 'Freak Season' Final Standings:

1.	Everton	42	20	13	9	102	66	53
2.	Huddersfield Town	42	22	7	13	91	68	51
3.	Leicester City	42	18	12	12	96	72	48
4.	Derby County	42	17	10	15	96	83	44
5.	Bury	42	20	4	18	80	80	44
6.	Cardiff City	42	17	10	15	70	80	44
7.	Bolton Wanderers	42	16	11	15	81	66	43
8.	Aston Villa	42	17	9	16	78	73	43
9.	Newcastle United	42	15	13	14	79	81	43
10.	Arsenal	42	13	15	14	82	86	41
11.	Birmingham	42	13	15	14	70	75	41
12.	Blackburn Rovers	42	16	9	17	66	78	41
13.	Sheffield United	42	15	10	17	79	86	40
14.	Sheffield Wednesday	42	13	13	16	81	78	39
15.	Sunderland	42	15	9	18	74	76	39
16.	Liverpool	42	13	13	16	84	87	39
17.	West Ham United	42	14	11	17	81	88	39
18.	Manchester United	42	16	7	19	72	80	39
19.	Burnley	42	16	7	19	82	98	39
20.	Portsmouth	42	16	7	19	66	90	39
21.	**Tottenham Hotspur**	**42**	**15**	**8**	**19**	**74**	**86**	**38**
22.	Middlesbrough	42	11	15	16	81	88	37

— VIVIAN WOODWARD,
GENTLEMAN FOOTBALLER —

Tottenham's fine footballing traditions go back a long way, and Vivian Woodward – one of the club's finest ever players and the first Tottenham Hotspur player to be capped for England – was among the earliest exponents of the style with which the club would become associated. He was a centre forward who relied on skill and guile in an age when most players in his position preferred brute force. He scored 75 goals in 171 appearances, but his game was as much about creating chances as scoring.

Vivian Woodward: The first Spurs player to play for England

Born in June 1879 in Kennington, South London, Woodward was an architect by profession, playing his football for Southern League Chelmsford City. The bigger clubs soon took notice and in 1901 he accepted an invitation to play for Spurs, still an amateur club. Business engagements prevented Woodward from making more than a handful of appearances in his first two seasons, but from 1902/03 onwards he turned out regularly and his career blossomed.

He was tall, slim and elegant, and possessed of an uncanny control of the ball, gliding past the full-blooded challenges of the days' defenders. He was soon called up by the international selectors, playing 67 amateur games for England and the United Kingdom, and 23 full internationals for England. He captained the UK teams that won the Olympic title in 1908 and 1912.

Woodward scored Spurs' first ever league goal on 1st September 1908 and was the club's top scorer in their first professional season, with 18 goals. By this time he was also a director, but shocked the club on the eve of the first season in the top flight by resigning to return to Chelmsford City. Another shock was to come when Woodard joined Chelsea just a few months later.

Although he was one of the most celebrated players of his time, Woodward never won a domestic honour. He came closest when he led Chelsea to the FA Cup Final in 1915 but refused to play, as to do so would have deprived Bob Thomson – whose goals had taken Chelsea to the final – of his place in the team.

— THE ONE AND ONLY MARTIN JOL —

Coming across like a Dutch football version of *The Sweeney's* Inspector Regan, Martin Jol has quickly become a cult hero among Tottenham fans. His coaching skills took Spurs to their best-ever Premiership finish in 2005/06, a feat he repeated in 2006/07 and he has charmed and entertained supporters, press and neutrals alike with his quick-witted (and occasionally curious) comments.

"It's not a case of me pleasing them, it's what they can do to please me. We pay their wages."
On being asked how he keeps his strikers happy.

"Stuart is probably still wearing the jumpers I sold him."
Jol confessed that he sold counterfeit designer wear to team-mates, including Stuart Pearce, when he was a Coventry player in the early 1980s.

"At the moment I am annoyed with Wenger, but I'm not a guy who holds a grudge and tomorrow, I will sit down and feel much more

calm about this. I won't have a problem with him in the future and I hope he is the same with me. I rate the guy, after all. All I can say is that when Wenger squared up to me on the touchline, I had to hold myself back because he doesn't know how strong I am."
After the last North London derby to be played at Highbury on April 22nd 2006.

"I always try to educate players. I think we have done well the last two seasons. We have no divers, we never provoke away crowds. We are an honest team and I hope in the future that will always be so."

"This is one of the biggest clubs in Europe and I want to be a part of its history."

"Defoe was nibbling his arm, but if you ask Mascherano to show you any marks on it he will not be able to. Mascherano had kicked Jermain from behind three times and Defoe wanted to show his frustration in a nice, comical way."
After Jermain Defoe was pictured biting Mascherano, then of West Ham, during a game in October 2006

"I can swear that it didn't happen. It's the same if you told my wife I'm gay. You'd have a big laugh. Nobody can change my mind or tell me what to do. Even the chairman would have a good laugh about it."
On reports that Jol had been instructed by a board member to select Dimitar Berbatov for a 2007 FA Cup game against Chelsea.

"I love the board members. They love me, we're good, getting on. They can talk about football. Even the chairman, he knows nothing about football but of course he has an opinion."

The gaffer

— WHITE HART LANE 2: THE EAST STAND —

"It is a wedding cake stand, shining with whiteness . . . It is a joy to behold, at once perfectly proportioned, yet apparently extraordinary," wrote author Simon Inglis in 1985 of the old East Stand. Even today, with a late 1980s makeover, it conjures up a unique atmosphere.

Originally a plain bank with a squat roof running most of its length, the East Stand was later expanded to allow more extensive terracing before, in 1934, development began on a brand new stand. Designed like the West Stand by Archibald Leitch, for the then huge cost of £60,000 Spurs got arguably the finest stand in the country, with a top tier of 5,100 seats, space for 11,000 standing supporters on the tier below (the finest terraced view in the country), and another 8,000-capacity terrace below that. Topped off with a large press box high up on the roof, and later with the re-sited cockerel statue and additional floodlights, the new East Stand was the jewel in White Hart Lane's crown.

Set just to right of centre along the middle tier was the famous 'Shelf', a section of terracing perched, like a shelf, between the upper seated-tier and the paddock below. Next to the Shelf was the 'Cage', a smaller section of terracing on the same mid-tier level, so called for being hemmed in by metal and wooden fences. From these two parts of the ground, the bulk of White Hart Lane's crowd noise was traditionally generated. But much of that atmosphere was lost when the refurbishment of the stand was completed in 1989. It was a controversial project, alienating many fans over the removal of the Shelf to make way for yet more executive boxes.

Gone also was the old roof and in came a vast new cover. The rear wall was not strong enough to support a cantilever, so instead huge, view-obstructing pillars had to be built to take the weight. The total cost of nearly £9m contributed to the club nearly going out of business in 1991, while a delay in its opening meant Spurs could not fulfil their opening fixture of the season against Coventry and the club were deducted two league points, changed to a £15,000 fine on appeal. When the stand was finally opened on the October 18th 1989, Spurs beat Arsenal 2–1.

Despite its impressive size the East Stand holds just 10,691 spectators and is notable for several curiosities in its history. During the Blitz it was used as a temporary morgue for victims of bombing raids, while police horses have been stabled in its depths. The old press box was reached by rickety lift and the high vantage point it provided was outstanding, but not recommended for anyone with vertigo.

— THE DOUBLE'S FIRST XI —

The opening sequence of 11 straight league wins at the start of the 1960/61 season was made up of the following games:

Date	Result	Scorers
Aug 20th	Tottenham 2 Everton 0	Smith R, Allen
Aug 22nd	Blackpool 1 Tottenham 3	Medwin, Dyson 2
Aug 27th	Blackburn Rovers 1 Tottenham 4	Smith R 2, Allen, Dyson
Aug 31st	Tottenham 3 Blackpool 1	Smith R 3
Sept 3rd	Tottenham 4 Manchester United 1	Smith R 2, Allen 2
Sept 7th	Bolton Wanderers 1 Tottenham 2	White, Allen
Sept 10th	Arsenal 2 Tottenham 3	Saul, Allen, Dyson
Sept 14th	Tottenham 3 Bolton Wanderers 1	Blanchflower (p) Smith R 2
Sept 17th	Leicester City 1 Tottenham 2	Smith R 2
Sept 24th	Tottenham 6 Aston Villa 2	Mackay, White 2, Smith R, Allen, Dyson
Oct 1st	Wolves 0 Tottenham 4	Blanchflower, Jones, Allen, Dyson

Spurs' run was ended by party poopers Manchester City who drew 1–1 at White Hart Lane in the 12th game of the season on October 10th 1960. Bill Nicholson's men eventually lost their unbeaten record on November 12th 1960, going down 2–1 to Sheffield Wednesday at Hillsborough. The club lost only seven games all season – three at home and four away – and drew just four. Top scorer in the league was centre forward Bobby Smith, with a total of 28 goals.

— SPURS LEGENDS: DANNY BLANCHFLOWER —

Danny Blanchflower: "The game is about glory".

For many Spurs fans, Danny Blanchflower is simply the greatest football man of all time. Dave Bowler, in his *Biography of a Visionary* (Victor Gollancz, 1997), wrote, 'Danny Blanchflower was innovative, an original thinker, an enigma who was much misunderstood.' At Spurs he holds a special place as the captain of the Double winners, and as the man who coined one of the most memorable football quotes ever, albeit one which has bequeathed subsequent Spurs teams a heavy burden.

"The game is about glory," he famously said. "It's about doing things in style, with a flourish. It's about going out and beating the other lot, not waiting for them to die of boredom.'

Signed in 1954 for £30,000 from Aston Villa, Blanchflower was one of the greatest attacking wing halves of all time. He read the game expertly, was a master of distribution and a born leader. His ability to make tactical decisions on the pitch often landed him in trouble, most famously when he was stripped of the Spurs captaincy after changing a player's position during the 1956 FA Cup semi-final.

When Bill Nicholson arrived, he gave Blanchflower carte blanche to run the show on the pitch, and the manager built his team around the talented Irishman.

At the start of the 1960/61 season, Blanchflower told club chairman Fred Bearman, "We'll do the Double this year." Spurs did precisely that, and Blanchflower secured another Footballer of the Year title to go with the one he had won in 1958. He won a record 56 caps for Northern Ireland, captaining his country to their most successful World Cup in 1958. Injured against Glasgow Rangers in 1962's European Cup campaign, Blanchflower never really recovered, and in 1963 he retired after making 337 appearances for the club.

He went on to forge a career as a respected football journalist, bringing his unique view of the world to bear in an engaging, witty and often provocative manner.

He was Nicholson's choice to take over as manager when Bill stepped down in 1974, but the club directors went for Terry Neill instead. The rumour was that they were not keen on Danny's independence. Instead, Blanchflower went on to manage Chelsea in 1978 but was not a success, something which he regretted but which enhanced his reputation among Spurs fans.

His lasting popularity comes not just because of his association with the romance of the Double winners, or his original thinking, but because he is a reminder of the simple pleasures football is supposed to bring, a kind of guardian of the game's soul. That was certainly biographer Dave Bowler's conclusion. He said, 'A game without joy, without hope, without ideals is bankrupt, morally and spiritually. British football needs a Danny Blanchflower, now more than ever. The pity of it is, it wouldn't know what to do with him.'

— CHAMPIONS 1961 —

Division One

	P	W	D	L	F	A	Pts
1. Tottenham Hotspur	42	31	4	7	115	55	66
2. Sheffield Wednesday	42	23	12	7	78	47	58
3. Wolverhampton Wanderers	42	25	7	10	103	75	57
4. Burnley	42	22	7	13	102	77	51
5. Everton	42	22	6	14	87	69	50
6. Leicester City	42	18	9	15	87	70	45
7. Manchester United	42	18	9	15	88	76	45
8. Blackburn Rovers	42	15	13	14	77	76	43
9. Aston Villa	42	17	9	16	78	77	43
10. West Bromwich Albion	42	18	5	19	67	71	41
11. Arsenal	42	15	11	16	77	85	41
12. Chelsea	42	15	7	20	98	100	37
13. Manchester City	42	13	11	18	79	90	37
14. Nottingham Forest	42	14	9	19	62	78	37
15. Cardiff City	42	13	11	18	60	85	37
16. West Ham United	42	13	10	19	77	88	36
17. Fulham	42	14	8	20	72	95	36
18. Bolton Wanderers	42	12	11	19	58	73	35
19. Birmingham City	42	14	6	22	62	84	34
20. Blackpool	42	12	9	21	68	73	33
21. Newcastle United	42	11	10	21	86	109	32
22. Preston North End	42	10	10	22	43	71	30

— THE DARKEST HOUR —

Arguably Tottenham's darkest hour was when, after scoring an average of 3.1 goals in the preceding games, Spurs were defeated 2–0 in the away leg of the 1973/74 UEFA Cup final against Feyenoord in Rotterdam, to lose 4–2 on aggregate.

The result, however, was overshadowed by serious fighting involving Spurs and Feyenoord fans and Dutch police. Despite an appeal from Bill Nicholson over the PA, disorder continued through much of the game. It was Tottenham's first defeat in 10 major cup finals and the violence played a major part in a disenchanted Nicholson resigning as boss.

As a result of the rioting, Spurs were ordered to play their next two European home games at least 250 kilometres from White Hart Lane. Spurs failed to qualify for the rest of the 1970s, and UEFA's 25th anniversary coincided with an amnesty for club sanctions, so the ban was never enforced.

— SPURS LEGENDS: DAVID GINOLA —

Caption: Yes he was worth it, actually . . .

In an era dominated by robotic box-to-box central midfielders, the truly artistic wide player has been a rare sighting in British football. It's some comfort, therefore, that arguably the last of this dazzling breed was a Spurs man.

David Ginola infuriated managers, charmed the media and was adored by the Tottenham faithful. Signed from Newcastle in the summer of 1997, he provided some much-needed glamour for a rather pedestrian Spurs side, and earned legions of female admirers with his Gallic looks and irresistible French allure that led to a string of advertising deals, notably for L'Oreal which provided him with a much-mocked catchphrase: 'Because I'm worth it'.

But Ginola was much more than a media darling. Fast, skilful, a brilliant reader of the game and devastating with his delivery, 'Daveeed's' exceptional talents delivered a Worthington Cup win in

1999 and earned him the PFA Players' Player of the Year award the same year. However, then manager George Graham's negative tactics ensured Ginola became an increasingly misused talent, exemplified by the former Arsenal boss leaving him out of a crucial UEFA Cup away leg in Kaiserslautern later in 1999. The die was cast and in July 2000, Ginola departed for Aston Villa.

Ginola played 127 games for Spurs and scored 22 goals, the pick of which was his Ricky-Villaesque waltz through entire Barnsley team as he scored the winner in a 1999 FA Cup quarter final. Like his compatriot and kindred spirit Eric Cantona, Ginola now stars as an actor. In May 2007, he made his big screen debut as Didier la Flore the butcher in the French romp *Rosbeef* – 'a tale of love, lust and a kilo of sausages'.

— UEFA CUP GLORY —

Tottenham's most recent victorious season in Europe saw the early 1980s side produce some of its finest performances. The 1983/84 UEFA Cup campaign began with a routine 14–0 aggregate demolition of Irish part-timers Drogheda, before Spurs renewed acquaintances with Feyenoord. This time, the encounter would be remembered solely for the quality of the football.

Spurs trounced the visitors 4–2 in the home leg (6–2 on agg.), scoring the goals in a first-half display many fans still regard as Glenn Hoddle's finest period of play. 'God' sprayed passes around at will, ably supported by his sorcerer's apprentice Mickey Hazard, Steve Archibald and Tony Galvin. The legendary Johan Cruyff played for the visitors that night but was totally overshadowed. (See *When Cruyff Met Hoddle*, page 111)

Revenge against the previous season's nemesis, Bayern Munich, and then victories over Austria Vienna and Hadjuk Split propelled Spurs into the final where they met Belgium's top side, Anderlecht (who featured Frank Arnesen among their ranks).

A tense 1–1 draw in the first leg in Brussels (Paul Miller was the Spurs scorer) was blighted by crowd trouble, with a young Tottenham fan shot dead by a trigger-happy bar owner prior to kick-off. Thankfully, there were no such problems at the return leg and attention was focused solely on the pitch.

In a nervy game of nip and tuck, neither side could fashion a breakthrough until Anderlecht, increasingly playing the more fluent football, took the lead through Alex Czerniatinski on the 60-minute mark.

The trophy was slipping away and for Keith Burkinshaw, in his last game as Spurs manager, there was one last throw of the dice. Off came Gary Mabbutt and Paul Miller, to be replaced by Ally Dick and Ossie Ardiles. With his first touch, the Argentinian cannoned a close range shot off the crossbar, but seconds later Graham Roberts muscled through the Anderlecht defence and scored the equaliser. There were just six minutes left on the clock.

Extra-time finished without further goals and so the final would be decided on penalties. Spurs could have won had Danny Thomas converted his effort (his spirits immediately lifted by a monumental chorus of 'One Danny Thomas' from the home fans), but redemption came seconds later as stand-in keeper Tony Parks sprang to his right and palmed away the spot-kick from Arnor Gudjohnsen (father of Barcelona's Eidur).

Spurs had won 4–3 on penalties, White Hart Lane shook with unbridled joy and Tottenham had their third European trophy. An unforgettable night had a poignant conclusion as Burkinshaw, dismayed by the creeping commercialisation at Spurs, bade farewell after nine superb years with the immortal words "there used to be a football club over there".

— CHIVERS IS THE STRONGEST LINK —

In 2001 Martin Chivers and Martin Peters braved the acid tongue of spiky quiz show hostess Anne Robinson when they appeared on a footballers' special edition of the popular TV programme *The Weakest Link*.

The two Spurs stars did extremely well, beating off competition from the likes of 1966 World Cup winner George Cohen, former Chelsea goalkeeper Peter Bonetti and legendary commentator Kenneth Wolstenholme to reach the final. Chivers just pipped Peters in the head-to-head between the two Martins, winning a £10,000 prize which he donated to a cancer charity.

— MAKE MINE A 99 —

Jimmy Greaves's transfer to Tottenham in November 1961 broke the then British transfer record, but manager Bill Nicholson ensured the goalscorer extraordinaire would not be saddled with the burden of being the first £100,000 footballer: Greaves was bought from AC Milan for £99,999.

— WATCH OUT, BEADLE'S ABOUT —

If you can get the measure of a club by its celebrity fans, then Tottenham's superiority to the former Dial Square FC is clear. Among the famous who have revealed their love of the Arsenal are annoying TV chef Ainsley Harriott, smug chat show host Clive Anderson and serial Hollywood flop-maker Kevin Costner. A smattering of nouveau bandwagon jumpers like David Schwimmer, The Appleton sisters and Val Kilmer also need to be taken into consideration.

Most embarrassingly for the club, world public enemy number one Osama Bin Laden was also outed as a devoted fan by the tabloids in 2001. Hilariously, the Arsenal board banned him from the ground. This must be a major blow to a man intent on avoiding capture by the armed forces and intelligence services of half the world's nations!

In contrast, famous Spurs fans include purveyor of fine gentleman's clothing Ted Baker, film critic extraordinaire Barry Norman and ground-breaking musicians Simon Raymonde, of the Cocteau Twins, and Jah Wobble – not forgetting cool-again Cockney tunesmiths Chas Hodges and Dave Peacock. Gertcha!

Throw in top TV actor Neil Pearson and rare groovemeister Norman Jay, both of whom regularly turn up to watch Spurs home and away, and the gap in class is clear.

Not forgetting Patsy Kensit, the fresh faced child star of TV ads for frozen peas who went on to become a movie actress, model, singer, and all-round uber celeb thanks to her rock'n'roll marriages. Through it all, she's stayed faithful to the Tottenham cause, thanks in large part to a dad who brought her up the Spurs way. Dido is probably Arsenal's closest equivalent, once described by acid-penned columnist Julie Burchill as 'pure evil'.

As Spurs fan Bruce Lee (not that one!) says in the 2004 book *We Are Tottenham*, 'It's no coincidence that Jeremy Beadle's an Arsenal fan and the old genius Peter Cook is Spurs.'

5 cool Spurs celebrity fans
Peter Cook
Barry Norman
Ted Baker
Norman Jay
Jah Wobble

5 embarrassing Arsenal celebrity fans
Jeremy Beadle
Ainsley Harriot
Clive Anderson
The Appleton sisters
Osama Bin Laden

— SPURS LEGENDS: JOHN CAMERON —

The first of Spurs' great Scots, John Cameron is the man who originally put Spurs on the road to greatness. Signed in 1898 from Everton, where he played as an amateur, the Ayr-born inside forward was the club's top scorer in his first season, netting 24 goals. The following season he took Spurs to their first championship, in the Southern League, and the year after scored the equaliser in the FA Cup final that allowed the club to lift the FA Cup for the first time.

It was Cameron's extensive contacts in the game, particularly in his native Scotland, that enabled him to assemble the first great Spurs team, and one that brought the club to national prominence. On the pitch he could distribute the ball as well as score, gaining a reputation as a clever player. He was clever off the pitch too, soon becoming secretary-manager of Spurs, and secretary of the Players and Trainers Union. He stopped playing in 1903, but continued in an administrative and managerial role until 1906, when he resigned.

— YAP, YAP, RABBIT, RABBIT —

The complete list of Cockney tunesmiths Chas 'n' Dave's Tottenham songs:

Ossie's Dream (1981)
Diamond line: 'We know you're gonna play a blinder, in de cup for Tottingham'

Tottenham, Tottenham (1982)
Diamond line: 'When we get them on the pitch at Wembley, we'll be entertaining you, oi oi!'

Hot Shot Tottenham (1987)
Diamond line: 'Richard Gough and Chrissy Waddle, Gary Mabbutt and Glenn Hoddle, And Danny all the goals are gonna be for you'

The Victory Song (1991)
Diamond line: 'In the north London Cup, they were only runners-up, cos they can't get the double up the Arsenal'

It's Lucky For Spurs When The Year Ends In One (1991)
Diamond line: 'We first won the cup when the century begun'

— FIRST INTERNATIONAL CAP —

The first Spurs player to win an international cap was John L Jones, who played for Wales against Ireland in February 1898.

— FIRST OVERSEAS TOUR —

The club's first foreign tour was undertaken in May 1905, to Austria and Hungary. The results were:

Date	Venue	Result
May 4th	Vienna	Homen Wart Club 0 Tottenham 6
May 7th	Vienna	Everton 2 Tottenham 0
May 10th	Vienna	Vienna Athletic Club 1 Tottenham 4
May 12th	Budapest	Buda Pesth Thorna 1 Tottenham 7
May 14th	Budapest	Testgyakorborora 1 Tottenham 12
May 16th	Prague	Everton 1 Tottenham 0
May 21st	Prague	Slavia 1 Tottenham 8

— LOYAL SUPPORTERS —

When Spurs were relegated to Division Two in 1977, the fans flocked to back their team, roaring the club back to the top flight at the first time of asking. During the season in the lower tier, Spurs' average home attendance was 33,417, the best in the division by 8,000 and better than all but six Division One sides.

They also drew huge crowds wherever they played, at a time when attendances were in decline. Away at Crystal Palace, 40,522 turned up; at Sunderland, 31,960; and at Brighton 32,647. Nine away games drew crowds of more than 25,000, and the total watching Spurs in the league that season was 1,156,399.

Spurs eventually finished third, securing the final promotion spot on the last day of the season. Like Brighton and Hove Albion, Spurs had 56 points, but the Lilywhites went up courtesy of a goal difference which bettered Albion's by nine, the margin by which Bristol Rovers had been hammered in October in front of 26,571 at White Hart Lane.

— 500th PLAYER —

When John Piercy came on as a substitute against Derby County on October 16th 1999 he became the 500th player to be used by Spurs in Football League or Premier League games. Spurs won 1–0.

— HARK THE HERALDS —

Local newspapers the *Tottenham and Edmonton Weekly Herald* and the *Wood Green and Southgate Weekly Herald* have long served the area and published a history of the club in 1921, *A Romance of Football*, which contained the following passage . . .

> *Like the little brook that ripples its way among the hills, grows into a sturdy stream, flows on through smiling fields and desert rocks, and finally expands into a mighty river, so has been the career of the famous Tottenham club.*

The book also contained various insights into the early years at the club, including:

- The original club badge – a large letter 'H' – was set on a scarlet shield.
- 'Northumberland Rovers' was once considered as a name for the fledgling club.
- Despite the social aspirations of many among the local population and the club's early followers, Tottenham had its fair share of troublemakers. "For one or two years a kind of guerrilla warfare was waged amongst rival classes of lads. Once, a 'Saint' was racing along the High Road to school when he was pushed by a 'Barker's Bulldog' through a brand new plate glass window of a provisions merchant and came to an unceremonious end in a tub of Danish lard."
- Owing to lack of funds, match balls were often in short supply for the early Spurs. "Never mind, lads," president and devout Christian John Ripsher would say, "the Lord will provide." And sure enough come the day of the game, Ripsher would arrive, carrying two match balls.
- When Spurs visited Luton in 1887, the home skipper commented upon the diminutive stature of his opponents. His counterpart John 'Jack' Jull responded "Wait till after the match, old man, before you say any more; schoolboys or not, we can beat you!" Spurs won 2–1.
- In the aftermath of the famous 1901 FA Cup victory, an anonymous local bricklayer grabbed the trophy and filled it with intoxicating liquour. On the train home, Lord Kinnaird, President of the FA was one of the first to take a long swig from said cup, despite being an avowed teetotaller. Such an incident proved, claimed the *Herald's* writers, that "the duke's son and the cook's son are numbered among the Spurs well-wishers."

— STILL RICKY VILLA . . . —

A moment of inspiration from manager Keith Burkinshaw led directly to one of the greatest FA Cup final moments of all time. In the 1981 final, Ricky Villa endured a miserable afternoon against Manchester City before being substituted. He trudged off the pitch, aware that his dream of success was crumbling in front of an audience that included many thousands back home in Argentina.

As the teams left the pitch at the end of the drawn game, captain Steve Perryman advised Burkinshaw not to select Ricky for the replay. Back in the dressing room, Villa was a forlorn figure. But, says Burkinshaw, "I don't know what it was, when I got to the dressing room I had a sixth sense that he'd have a big part to play. He was down in the dumps, so I said, 'Ricky, get your head up. You're playing on Thursday.' He was so happy."

The rest is FA Cup history, Villa scoring two goals as Spurs won 3–2, the second a mesmerising, mazy run through the ranks of City's defence to slot home the goal John Motson has described as the best ever scored at Wembley.

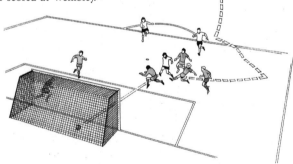

The greatest FA Cup final goal of all time

— LORD ARCHIBALD —

Sports psychologist John Syer was brought in to work with the Spurs team in 1991 by Keith Burkinshaw and physio Mike Varney. The players were initially suspicious, but gradually began to see the benefits of Syer's methods. Part of Syer's technique involved visualisation, which involved asking players to describe how they felt when doing certain things on the pitch. When Steve Archibald was quizzed about how he felt when going past opposing defenders his response was somewhat unexpected. "Like the Lord of the Manor," he said.

— DODGY SIGNINGS XI —

Spurs endured some lean years through the 1990s and into the early Noughties, and a scan of the club's transfer deals reveals why. In the wilderness years, the club which had once signed Jimmy Greaves, Gary Lineker, Jürgen Klinsmann, Ossie Ardiles and Ricky Villa, signed this lot . . .

1. **Willem Korsten** (2000)
2. **Ben Thatcher** (2000)
3. **Erik Edman** (2004)
4. **Dean Richards** (2001)
5. **Goran Bunjevcevic** (2001)
6. **Milenko Acimovic** (2002)
7. **Kazuyuki Toda** (2003)
8. **Stephane Dalmat** (2003)
9. **Mbelelo Mabizela** (2003)
10. **Timothee Atouba** (2004)
11. **Sergei Rebrov** (2000)

— NOT FAR TO TRAVEL —

On April 22nd 1944, Spurs played away against Arsenal – at White Hart Lane! The fixture was in the wartime Football League South, and with Highbury requisitioned for the war effort, Spurs were able to pay their neighbours back for the use of Highbury during the First World War. White Hart Lane had been used as a rifle range and gas mask factory during WWI, with Spurs alternately playing at Arsenal and Clapton Orient's grounds.

— 10 WONDERFULLY NAMED TOUR OPPONENTS —

Opposition	Date	Result
Testgyakorborora (Hungary)	May 14th 1905	Won 12–1
Wacker (Germany)	May 20th 1911	Won 8–1
Bewegungs Spiele (Germany)	May 16th 1912	Won 3–1
Zurich Young Fellows (Switzerland)	May 10th 1925	Won 2–0
La Chaux de Fonds (Switzerland)	May 20th 1925	Won 8–1
Saskatchewan FA (North America)	May 28th 1952	Won 18–1
Pecs Dozsa (Hungary)	May 20th 1955	Won 1–0
Rot-Weiss Essien (West Germany)	July 23rd 1972	Drew 1–1
St Jordal Blink (Norway)	July 27th 1984	Won 9–0.
Lansi Uudenmaan District X1	Aug 1st 1987	Won 7–2

— DIAMOND GEEZERS —

In 1987 Tottenham stars Chris Waddle and Glenn Hoddle released a pop song, *Diamond Lights,* which reached number 12 in the charts. The pair, who recorded the duet as 'Glenn and Chris', even got to appear on *Top of the Pops* – a performance which, alas, has gone down in the annals of pop for the atrocious pair of jumpers the duo were wearing.

In January 2004 the song was ranked at number 33 in a poll of the all-time worst pop singles voted by Channel Four viewers. Later that year *Diamond Lights* climbed to number four in a similar poll conducted by the food company Mars. Yet, incredibly, this was not the highest Spurs–related entry, as *Fog on the Tyne* by Paul Gascoigne and Lindisfarne was voted the second most nauseating song in pop history behind The Beatles' *Ob-La-Di, Ob-La-Da*. Hmm, sounds like that particular poll was hijacked by Arsenal fans . . .

— PUSH AND RUN MAGIC —

As the winter of 1950 drew in, Arthur Rowe's newly promoted Spurs side were creating a stir with their 'push and run' football, a style which relied on players passing quickly and accurately and then moving into space. It had swept them to the Second Division title and, despite a slightly shaky start, propelled them on a run of seven consecutive wins by the time league leaders Newcastle United visited White Hart Lane. This was the big test – the newcomers with their innovative system against the giants of the age who led the top-flight thanks largely to a defence that was considered invincible.

On November 18th 1950 more than 70,000 came to see if 'push and run' had a future, and many thousands more were locked out. By the end of the afternoon those massed inside had witnessed the dawning of a new football age.

Spurs mesmerised the Magpies, opening the scoring after five minutes and completing a 7–0 victory thanks to a penalty from Alf Ramsey in the dying seconds of the game. The result was greeted with astonishment in the football world, and Spurs went on to win the league title. 'Push and run' changed the face of football, showing that success was possible through movement, flair and adventure, rather than through the trusted but tired philosophies of hoof and dribble that characterised the English game. Rowe's bold experiment proved a successful formula and laid the groundwork to bring the domestic game out of its conservative inertia.

— LET'S BE FRANK —

After Spurs beat Arsenal 2–0 at White Hart Lane in 1981, their first derby win in five years, BBC1's *Match of the Day* revealed that Arsenal managerTerry Neill was tracking Danish international Frank Arnesen. Neill didn't get him, or Johan Cruyff who was also linked in the same report, but years later Arnesen briefly joined Spurs as Director of Football, before leaving to make tea for Jose Mourinho at Chelsea.

— THE WIT AND WISDOM OF DANNY BLANCHFLOWER —

"Now keep your heads and let's get going after a goal. We don't want that business down in our goalmouth again."
To the team at Roker Park after a fanatical home crowd had burst onto the pitch after their team equalised in an FA Cup tie in 1961.

"The trouble with you is you think you know all the answers."
Spurs director to Blanchflower
"Ah, God love you. You don't even know the questions."
Blanchflower's reply

"How do we bring the crowds back to football? Easy. Let them in for nothing and charge them to get out!"

"Blanchflower, you're finished!"
Young Nobby Stiles after upending Blanchflower
"Excuse me son, I haven't read the programme yet. What's your name?"
Blanchflower's reply

At the 1961 FA Cup final, Royal guest the Duchess of Kent pointed out that the Leicester players had their names on their tracksuits, while Tottenham's didn't. Blanchflower replied, "Yes Ma'am, but we all know one another."

"These teams can't play."
Blanchflower commentating on an early NASL game for US TV
"Accentuate positive truths rather than negative truths."
Producer
"These teams positively can't play."
Blanchflower

"All those social climbers and gadabouts at Wembley on Cup Final day at the expense of the long-suffering supporters."
Blanchflower on Cup Final ticket allocations in 1961

"I don't know who is going to win. That's why they're playing the match."
Blanchflower destroys the BBC's pre-match analysis spot before the 1964 FA Cup Final

"What exactly do you mean by a long ball? How does a long ball roll?"
Exasperating Spurs manager Jimmy Anderson

"It's all downhill from here."
To Bill Nicholson after Spurs thrashed Everton 10–4 in Nicholson's first game in charge

"We always equalise before the opposition."
Explaining Northern Ireland's successful run in the 1958 World Cup

— NOT SO SOLID CREWE —

Tottenham's fans have often been accused of being too pessimistic about their team, and an illustration of this trait came in February 1960 before a fourth round FA Cup replay when a local butcher painted the prediction 'Spurs 7 Crewe 0' on his window. In fact, the side ran up its biggest ever win in a first-class game, 13–2!

Spurs were smarting from being held to a draw at Gresty Road in the first game, and tore into their opponents from the off. By half time it was 10–1 to the Lilywhites, with goals raining in from headers, volleys, tap-ins, diving headers and dribbles. The scoring finished on 79 minutes when Cliff Jones converted from the penalty spot. While Spurs were dazzling, Crewe never gave up, constantly trying to make the scoreline at least a little more respectable. A crowd of 64,365 witnessed the record, which included five goals from Les Allen.

— IT'S RAINING GOALS —

When Spurs spanked Charlton 5–1 at White Hart Lane on December 9th 2006, it was the first time in 57 outings that the team had scored more than three goals in a game – the previous victims of a heavy thrashing being Aston Villa who went down 5–1 in April 2005. What's more Dimitar Berbatov, with a brace of goals, became the first Spurs player to score more than once in a game since Robbie Keane bagged both Spurs' goals in a 2–1 home win against WBA on March 27th 2006.

— GREAVSIE'S GOALS —

Jimmy Greaves was the First Division's top scorer for Spurs on four occasions, including three in succession between 1963–65.

Season	Greaves' Total	Tottenham's total
1961/62	21	88
1962/63	37	111
1963/64	35	97
1964/65	29	87
1965/66	15	75
1966/67	25	71
1967/68	23	70
1968/69	27	61

— AND SO THIS IS CHRISTMAS —

Spurs may have disappointed fans with a haul of just four points from the 12 on offer over Christmas 2006, but just as turkeys don't like Christmas, the cockerel has rarely strutted its stuff over the festive period.

In the 95 Christmas programmes Spurs have participated in since joining the league, they have achieved a Scrooge-like average of 3.83 points per Christmas – collecting just 364 points from the 718 on offer. And in the 15 seasons since the Premiership started, Spurs have taken a mere four points from 12 on four occasions, and a hardly festive four from nine a further four times.

However, it hasn't been all bad. In 1961/62, Spurs recorded two wins over Chelsea on consecutive days, when the Christmas programme regularly featured back-to-back matches. On December 23rd, Jimmy Greaves and Cliff Jones scored the goals which beat Chelsea 2–0 at Stamford Bridge, and the next day Jones got a hat-trick and Dave Mackay and Les Allen another two in a 5–1 Christmas turkey shoot. And on the most special Christmas Day of all, December 25th 1911, a crowd of 47,109 saw Spurs beat Woolwich Arsenal 5–0. Now that's a Christmas cracker!

— SAY IT AIN'T SO, SOL —

Much has been said and written about the decision of former Spurs skipper Sol Campbell to switch to Arsenal in 2001. Here is what happened, in his own words.

"My heart and soul is here and I want to play for Spurs. I am going nowhere – for now."
August 4th 2000

"I can assure everyone that I won't be signing for another club while I am still a Spurs player. I want to win the Premiership and I want success in Europe but, most of all, I want to believe I can achieve that here."
December 3rd 2000

"Being a Spurs fan as a boy and a player for so many years, it would be hard to sign for Arsenal. I don't think the fans here would ever forgive me."
December 17th 2000

"I want to play for Tottenham, that's it really. I am going nowhere."
January 1st 2001

"I'm happy here and willing to do business now. I'm not selfish, I'm looking at the current situation and I want the club to do well."
January 5th 2001

"It's the ambition of Spurs and where we are going that concerns me. I have the right to keep my options open. Nobody can blame me for wanting success and above all wanting it at Tottenham. But talk is cheap."
March 11th 2001

"As long as the club is healthy and things are in place, then myself and other players will want to join Tottenham or continue with them. I want to stay at Tottenham."
March 26th 2001

"There is still a lot of sorting out to be done, but I am sure it will be resolved."
April 1st 2001

"I will leave it as late as possible – but I am happy at the moment and that's the main thing."
April 13th 2001

"Going abroad is not in my mind. The ball is in Spurs' court now. I am in no hurry because I want to look at the whole picture. We will just have to wait and see what happens in the next two or three weeks."
May 21st 2001

Sol Campbell signs for Arsenal on a Bosman free transfer.
July 3rd 2001

— NAME THAT TEAM —

Nicknames have long been popular with both fans and players, but can you guess the real names of this first eleven of nicknamed Tottenham first-teamers?

Helen, The Ginger Pele, Ferrero, Wipey, The Cheeky Girls, Sicknote, Max, God, Boutros Boutros, Rocket

Answers: Kasey Keller, Gary Doherty, Riccardo Rocha, Lee Young-Pyo, Goran Bunjevcevic and Milenko Acimovic, Darren Anderton, Paul Miller, Glenn Hoddle, Hossam Ghaly, Ronnie Rosenthal.

— THE ADVENTURES OF GAZZA —

Some of the pranks Paul Gascoigne got up to during his colourful Spurs career include:

Inviting his friends (including Jimmy 'Five Bellies' Gardner) to stay at the 5-star West Lodge Hotel in Hertfordshire during negotiations over his move to Spurs, all at the club's expense. After a weekend of champagne-fuelled mayhem that included Gardner taking a naked dip in the hotel's ornamental fishpond, Gascoigne and Gardner told a forgiving chairman Irving Scholar, "thank you for the best weekend of our lives."

While out on the town with his Tottenham colleague Gary Lineker, Gascoigne commandeered a London bus and drove it for a few yards near Piccadilly Circus. Gascoigne had ensured Lineker had joined the bemused passengers.)

Walking into a newsagent on a trip back to his native Gateshead, leaving £500 behind the counter and asking the shop owner to 'buy some sweets for the local kids.'

Inviting a Spurs fan to sit on the roof of his stationary car – and then setting off (within the speed limit of course) with the petrified fan hanging on the roof for dear life.

On driving past some roadworks, Gazza jumped out and asked one of the workman if he could 'have a go' with his pneumatic drill. And he did, proceeding to pound the pavement with enthusiasm.

For the World Cup in 1990, each player had to film a short piece of footage to be used whenever team line ups were given before each game. Gascoigne mouthed the words 'f***ing w****r' and each time it was shown, the nation's lip readers were given a pre-watershed blast of profanity.

— CROSSING THE DIVIDE —

Given the geographical proximity (3.3 miles) of the two clubs, it is perhaps surprising that only 21 players thus far have played for both Spurs and Arsenal. Then again, given the intense rivalry, it is perhaps surprising that so many have chosen to risk incurring the fans' wrath. Here, in chronological order, are the footballers who have crossed the great North London divide.

The rescued: Arsenal to Tottenham
Lycurgus Burrows (1894)
Tom Hatfield (1896)
Tom Meade (1897)
Walter Bugg (1902)
James Brain (1931)
Ron Piper (1960)
Laurie Brown (1964)
David Jenkins (1968)
Pat Jennings (1985)
Rohan Ricketts (2002)

The lost: Tottenham to Arsenal
David Black (1898)
Peter Kyle (1906)
George Hunt (1937)
Freddie Cox (1949)
Jimmy Robertson (1968)
Willie Young (1977)
Kevin Stead (1977)
Steve Walford (1977)
Pat Jennings (1977)
Narada Bernard (1999)
Sol Campbell (2001)

— INTO THE LYON'S DEN —

There were extraordinary scenes in the first leg of Tottenham's European Cup Winners Cup tie in Lyon on November 30th 1967 as players and fans fought on the pitch.

It was a tough game from the start, with Olympique Lyonnais body-checking and tough tackling. On 33 minutes, Alan Mullery tackled Lyon hard-man Andre Guy. Both players went to ground, but as they rose Guy kicked Mullery full in the face. The Spurs team sprinted to help the now prostrate Mullery and were intercepted by the Lyon players streaming from every area of the pitch to join battle with fists and feet. As blows were swapped, dozens of French fans spilled on to the pitch to join the fray. Chaos reigned for eight minutes before referee Josef Krnavek gave Guy and Mullery, who had risen to punch his assailant, red cards.

Violence flared again in the tunnel at half-time as the brooding Guy lunged at Alan Gilzean, catching Bill Nicholson in the eye with an elbow as the manager intervened. A ten-a-side punch-up followed as Guy screamed abuse at Mullery through the dressing-room door.

Spurs lost the game 1–0, and went out on away goals after a 4–3 victory at White Hart Lane in the return.

— SWISS ROLLED —

In May 1925 Spurs toured Switzerland, playing seven games in which they scored 29 goals and conceded only two.

Date	Opposition	Score
May 9th	v Basle Old Boys	3–0 (Thompson, Lane, Dimmock)
May 10th	v Zurich Young Fellows	2–0 (Seed, Hanley)
May 17th	v Winterthur	4–0 (Seed 2, Lane, Dimmock)
May 18th	v Lausanne	6–1 (Handley 3, Dimmock, 3)
May 20th	v La Chaux de Fonds	8–1 (Richardson, Smith, White, Landsay, Handley 3, Dimmock)
May 21st	v Berne	5–0 (Clay, Lindsay 3, Dimmock)
May 24th	v Basle	1–0 (Lindsay)

— NEIGHBOURS —

In the days before the wage cap for players was lifted, many clubs used to buy houses which they would rent to married players – just as owners in industry had traditionally established tied housing for their employees. This meant the club could establish a property portfolio, earn rental income and offer a stable domestic background to their players.

Tottenham Hotspur owned a row of six in Roedean Avenue, Enfield. At one stage in the fifties Eddie Baily, Ron Burgess, Les Stevens and Ernie Jones all lived there alongside one another.

— A SPURS PLAYER WALKS INTO A PUB . . . —

Footballers and football fans have all been known to like the odd tipple from time to time. These days, players tend to socialise only in those watering holes where paparazzi and female soap stars are in attendance, with *Faces* in Ilford a popular haunt, but in years past the following local hostelries have provided many an opportunity for happy celebrations or drowning of sorrows.

The Players' Social Club
Situated on the corner of White Hart Lane and Tottenham High Road, the social club was more of a snooker hall than pub, and played host to a generation of footballers around the turn of the 20th century. Flat caps and brown ale were the order of the day, and in honour of the various home nationalities of the squad, English, Scottish, Welsh and Irish flags were hung from the ceiling.

The Bell and Hare
A large Edwardian pub just around the corner from the stadium on the High Road, The Bell and Hare's regulars included most of the Double side and, more frequently than not, Jimmy Greaves. "We'd go in the Bell and Hare after matches," he said, "loads of players, few fans, bunch of press lads. All in the back room of the pub. We'd have a good few drinks, knowing the fans would be no trouble and the press wouldn't turn us over." Now a heaving match-day pub for home fans only.

The Coolbury Club
Another High Road establishment. Patrons included Glenn Hoddle and many of the 1981 FA Cup winning squad.

Charlie Chan's
Habitual hangout for Teddy Sheringham and assorted footballers, Charlie Chan's location at Walthamstow Greyhound Stadium provides all the modern pro could possibly want on a night out under one roof: namely, betting, boozing and plenty of aspiring Page Three girls.

Epping Forest Country Club
Chigwell's late, lamented premier nitespot. Regulars included Teddy Sheringham, while football nut Rod Stewart was known to pop his head round the door.

— PICK THAT OUT! —

When goalkeeper Ted Ditchburn missed the game against Sunderland on March 20th 1954, it brought his remarkable run of 247 consecutive league appearances to an end. Spurs lost the game 3–0. Ditchburn's run, set between April 17th 1948 and March 17th 1954, is still a club record for consecutive appearances.

Amazingly, Ditchburn's record is some way short of the record for most consecutive league appearances, which is held by Tranmere Rovers' Harold Bell. Between 1946 and 1955, Bell racked up an astonishing 401 appearances in a row.

— ALTERNATIVE TV —

Spurs famously became the first team from the modern era to win the league and cup double in 1960/61, but what's less well known is that, in the same season, the club turned down the chance to be one of the first to feature live on TV.

At the start of the season the Football League agreed a £150,000 deal to show 26 league games live on ITV. Selected games would kick off at 6.50pm on Saturdays, and a programme called *The Big Game* would begin at 7.30pm. This would allow the channel to show the final minutes of the first half, open up a lucrative ad spot during half time, and then show the second half in its entirety.

On September 10th 1960, Blackpool v Bolton became the first league game shown live on British TV, complete with colour commentary from a celebrity footballer, Billy Wright. The scheduled game the following week was Arsenal v Newcastle, but the Arsenal board refused the cameras entry; as did the Spurs board for the game against Aston Villa on September 24th.

Football League Secretary Alan Hardaker had, it became clear, agreed a deal without the authority of the club chairmen. ITV withdrew the offer, and the BBC also took its offer of £45,000 for six FA Cup ties off the table. So Spurs played a leading role in delaying football's TV revolution by three decades. Had they not done so they would have won the historic Double in the full glare of the cameras, establishing themselves as England's pre-eminent club at the start of a period of unprecedented publicity and riches. Instead, by the time the Sky TV deal changed the game fundamentally, helped ironically enough by the chairman of Tottenham Hotspur, the club was no longer even one of the Big Five.

— SPURS LEGENDS: GARY MABBUTT —

In the modern era of agents and freedom of contract, long-serving players have become a rare breed. Gary Mabbutt was an exception to that rather dispiriting rule. In 16 fantastic years at White Hart Lane, 11 of them as club captain, Mabbutt resisted the temptation to sign for other clubs and stayed loyal to the Spurs cause, battling against injury and career-threatening illness to establish himself as a Tottenham great.

As a diabetic Mabbutt was advised by doctors that a career as a professional footballer was not an option. Gary proved them wrong and followed his father Ray and brother Kevin into the Bristol Rovers team, winning England Youth and Under-21 honours. Feeling he'd reached a ceiling at Rovers, Mabbutt wrote to every First Division club requesting they give him a chance. Impressing the sharp eye of Bill Nicholson at a trial game, Mabbutt signed for Spurs on August 11th 1982 for a modest fee of £105,000.

Mabbutt never looked back. He swiftly established himself as a key member of the Spurs side, not least because he was so versatile – nicknamed for a time 'The Bionic Man' for his superhuman energy and commitment – and over the years played in virtually every position except goalkeeper. Honours soon followed. He won the first of 16 England caps against West Germany in 1982 and earned a UEFA Cup winners medal in 1984. Established as a centre-half by David Pleat in 1986, 'Mabbsie' took the captain's armband a year later, though the season ended on a note of failure when, having earlier put Spurs ahead, Gary was the unlucky scorer of the own goal that enabled Coventry to defeat Spurs in the FA Cup final.

Four years later, redemption came when Gary lifted the famous trophy as Spurs beat Nottingham Forest. It was just reward for years of loyal service; despite offers from Liverpool and Manchester United and a general sense of underachievement for Tottenham, Mabbutt stuck by the club. He suffered for the cause, breaking a leg against Blackburn in the first game of the 1996/97 season that ruled him out of the campaign, and suffering a shattered cheekbone and eye socket in 1993 after a brutal challenge from Wimbledon's John Fashanu. Awarded the MBE while he was recovering (he later wore a protective *Phantom-of-the-Opera*-style mask), Mabbutt said, "When I saw my face, I looked like the Elephant Man," adding with characteristic understatement, "Fashanu was not playing with due care and attention."

Modest, friendly, honest and a true gentleman, Gary Mabbutt played 585 games for Spurs between 1982 and 1998, scoring 38 goals. To this day, when engaged in media work he still describes Spurs as 'we' and 'us'. Legend status is thus assured.

— KEEP IT IN THE FAMILY —

Is football genius in the genes? These Tottenham family connections may help you decide.

The Casey family: brothers Lindsay and Hamilton (aka Ham or Sam) were two of the original local lads who met underneath the lamp-post on the High Road to form the club in the summer of 1882. Their father supplied the first goalposts which were painted blue and white – appropriate given the club's modern colours but something of a curiosity given that the first colours Spurs played in were all navy blue.

The Allens: Dad Les was a league and FA Cup winner with Bill Nick's immortal Double side; son Clive banged in a club record 49 goals in the extraordinary 1986/87 season and is now manager of the reserve side; cousin Paul became the youngest ever FA Cup final winner (with West Ham) in 1980, spent nine years at Spurs and is now a matchday host at White Hart Lane.

Chris, Leon and Cian Hughton: Chris was one of Tottenham's finest full-backs, winning FA Cup medals in 1981 and 1982 and a UEFA Cup medal in 1984, featuring for 11 years as a player and, to date, 13 years as a coach. Son Leon did not make a first team appearance and is now at Hoddesdon Town, but younger brother Cian is currently on Spurs' books.

Glenn and Carl Hoddle: When you're the younger brother of arguably the most gifted English player since the Second World War, it's tough to make a name for yourself. After Carl was released by Spurs (described by Glenn as one of his saddest days in football) he set off on a career that took in, amongst others, Barnet, Leyton Orient and Enfield Town.

Pat Jennings and Pat Jennings jnr: The world's greatest shot-stopper with the giant hands was Tottenham's man between the sticks for 590 games, scoring one goal. Son Patrick had a brief association as a Spur before taking up goalkeeping duties with, among others, League of Ireland sides UCD and Derry City.

The Henrys: Ron won the league, two FA Cups and a European Cup Winners Cup and his son Steve figured in the youth team of the early 1970s. Grandson Ronnie played for the schoolboys.

The Howells: Midfielder David played alongside his goalkeeping brother Gareth in the Tottenham youth team and went on to earn an FA Cup winners medal in 1991. Gareth didn't progress to the first team and went on to play for Torquay United and was recently turning out for non-league Aldershot.

Ray and Stephen Clemence: Son Stephen may not have emulated his father's international and trophy winning exploits with Spurs and Liverpool but is one of the few players to have matched his father's record in playing in the top flight of British football, first at Spurs, later at Birmingham City. Of his early playing days as the son of a famous father, Steve said, "When I started doing quite well with youth teams at county level, my dad tried to stay away from the games. If he was there everyone would know I was playing and that would put added pressure on me. My dad wouldn't let me join Tottenham until I was 13 even though the club had wanted me since I was nine or ten."

— SITUATIONS VACANT —

Nowadays, footballers appear as fully-fledged world stars at ever more tender ages, knowing nothing of the world aside from kicking a ball and having a photogenic girlfriend. Once upon a time, footballers used to do proper jobs before fame came to call.

Chris Hughton: Lift engineer
Terry Naylor: Porter at Smithfield meat market
Graham Roberts: Fitters mate
Ossie Ardiles: Law graduate
Paul Stewart: Roofing contractor
Terry Venables: Wig designer, singer (two sidelines of 'El Tel' while he was at Chelsea)
Pat Jennings: Worked in a timber yard in Newry

— BOWLED OVER —

Bill Edrich was one of England's finest-ever cricketers, and still holds the record for the second highest average in a single English season, alongside Denis Compton. But between 1935 and 1937 Edrich played 20 games of football for Tottenham Hotspur as an amateur. An outside-left, he managed four goals for the club before giving up football to concentrate full time on cricket.

Norfolk-born Edrich, who also turned out for Norwich City, continued his first-class cricket career until 1958, chalking up 571 matches. A right arm fast bowler and attacking right-handed batsman, he took 479 first-class wickets and scored 36,965 runs. He was named Wisden Cricketer of the Year in 1940, and captained Middlesex and Norfolk CCCs. During the Second World War he rose to the rank of squadron leader, and won the DFC.

He died at his home in Chesham in 1986, aged 70. Today, one of the twin stands at the Nursery End at Lords bears his name. The other bears the name of Denis Compton, who he captained Middlesex with in 1951 and 52, and the only man to record a higher season's average. Compton, of course, was also a handy outside-left, plying his footballing skills at Arsenal.

— PERSONAL COLUMN —

Some 'highlights' from various player profiles in the match programme and *Shoot!* magazine

Mark Bowen
Ambition outside game: To get a drink from Ally Dick
Tony Galvin
Favourite holiday resort: Blackpool
Miscellaneous likes: *Tiswas*
Peter Southey
Hobbies outside of football: Carpentry
Glenn Hoddle
Pets: A greyhound called Chris's Babe

— BUTCHER, BAKER, CANDLESTICK MAKER —

Among the former Spurs stars who have gone on to excel at other things are.

Terry Naylor: Postman
Martin Peters: Insurance company owner
John Pratt: Cleaning company owner
Dave Mackay: Tie shop owner
Terry Venables: Crime writer, nightclub owner, board game designer, TV pundit, football club owner, national team manager
Paul Miller: Investment banker
Pat van de Hauwe: Gardener
Ricky Villa: Ranch owner
Jamie Redknapp: Magazine publisher
Gary Brooke: Football statistics analyst
Ruel Fox: Restaurateur
Willie Young: Publican
Frank Saul: Builder
Tony Galvin: College lecturer
Gerry Francis: Theatre impresario and pigeon expert
David Ginola: Actor
Mickey Hazard: Taxi driver
Mark Kendall: Policeman
John Lacy: Home improvements salesman
Paul Moran: Painter and decorator
Gica Popescu: Football agent
Danny Blanchflower: Journalist
Alan Gilzean: Transport manager
Bobby Smith: Painter and decorator

— ON-SCREEN OSSIE —

The history of footballers in the movies is not a distinguished one, but Spurs legend Osvaldo Ardiles gave an Oscar-worthy display in the cult film *Escape To Victory* (1981). Ok, he may have not had much of a speaking part, but his portrayal of Rey, the midfield dynamo in the team of plucky Allied POWs that triumphs over a crack German armed forces side, was surely on a par with Laurence Olivier's *Hamlet*. The highlight came when Ossie executed in glorious slo-mo his trademark trick: flicking the ball over his opponent's head before collecting the ball to leave the defender completely flummoxed.

— TERRY'S CRAFTY FLUTTER —

Whatever the outcome of the 1967 FA Cup final between Tottenham and his previous club Chelsea, Spurs midfielder Terry Venables was in a 'win-win' situation, as he later recalled.

"I was in a betting shop around Christmas 1966 with Dave Mackay, Alan Gilzean and Jimmy Robertson. I looked up on the wall and I saw Chelsea were 25–1 to win the FA Cup and I felt that would just be my luck – they'd gone close twice whilst I was there. So I had £25 on Chelsea, which was a lot of money in those days, to win. So, we get to the final – Tottenham – and who do we play? Chelsea. And in my contract for Tottenham it's £500 to win (the cup). So, I'm on £500 to win and £500 to lose. In actual fact, it was better for me to lose because you had to pay tax for the money in the contract but not in those days on betting. Obviously, though, I wanted to win and a 2–1 victory did the trick for us."

And also for the bookie, who didn't have to pay out on Tel's bet.

— FRENCH BETTER —

Years before Ardiles and Villa, Spurs were looking abroad for talent. In 1913 the club made an attempt to sign French amateur international goalkeeper Chayrigues, of Red Star Amical. The decision appears to have been a strange one, as Tottenham had thumped 11 goals past him in two tour matches played in Paris in May 1913, but he must have had something about him as the London club offered him a contract. But in the end, Chayrigues never turned out in Spurs colours.

— PAYING THEIR DUES —

For many years Tottenham Hotspur FC had a policy of not granting players testimonials. However, the club did take part in games which benefited players of other teams, and also in tribute games for Spurs players whose careers had been brought to an early or tragic end. Most notable was the memorial for the great John White, who had been struck by lightning and killed whilst playing golf aged just 26, when Spurs played a Scotland X1 on November 11th 1964. Scotland ran out winners against a Spurs line-up of W Brown, Baker, Henry, Mullery, L.Brown, Marchi, Robertson, Greaves, T White, Jones and Dyson.

In the early 1970s the policy was changed, with Jimmy Greaves the first beneficiary with a match against Feyenoord on October 17th 1972. Spurs won 2–1, lining up with Daines, Evans, Knowles, Coates (Holder), England (Naylor), Beal, Gilzean (Pearce), Perryman, Chivers, Greaves, Peters.

— CLASSIC MATCHES 4: AN ELECTRIFYING 90 MINUTES —

Spurs 2   **Benfica 1** (Benfica win 4–3 on agg.)
Smith   Aguas
Blanchflower (pen)

April 5th 1962: European Cup, semi-final second leg
White Hart Lane
Att: 64,448

Tottenham's first foray into European football reached an unforgettable climax in a classic semi-final encounter with Benfica. Many agreed that this was in effect the final: the titanic showdown between the two best sides in the competition, pitting the proven pedigree of the Portuguese champions against the dash and verve of the best club side England had ever produced.

The two matches did not disappoint. In the first tie in Lisbon, goals from Aguas and Augusto (2) established a 3–1 advantage, with Bobby Smith's strike keeping Tottenham in contention. Had two highly contentious offside decisions not gone against Spurs, the score would have been 3–3, but Nicholson refused to blame the officials and instead offered up errors by his own players by way of explanation. With Spurs determined to remedy such mistakes the stage was thus set for a return leg of genuinely epic proportions.

Grown men still go misty-eyed at the recollection of an unforgettable night at White Hart Lane. Driven on by a ceaseless, deafening wall of noise (author and fan Phil Soar described it as 'terrifying' in *Tottenham Hotspur: The Official History* (Hamlyn, 1995), Spurs laid siege to the Benfica rearguard. An early goal for the visitors from Aguas might have punctured lesser sides, but Spurs roared back. Yet another goal was disallowed as Greaves was ruled offside, but a strike from Smith and then a Blanchflower penalty four minutes after the break gave Spurs ample time to get the two goals they needed.

Some, including winger Cliff Jones, felt that Tottenham's approach was too hasty, at a cost to the team's silkier style, but Nicholson's astute tactical nous in fielding what was a then revolutionary 4-3-3 formation enabled his side to sustain unrelenting pressure. Wave after wave of attack was launched, and three times in the second half Spurs hit the woodwork as shots rained in on the Benfica goal.

But it was not to be. At the final whistle, both sets of players collapsed into each other's arms. There were no spiteful recriminations, no graceless outbursts of false hurt designed to cloud individual failings, just a mutual respect for each other's endeavours. This, truly, was sport of the highest calibre.

The *Daily Express*'s David Miller described it 20 years later as 'the most electrifying 90 minutes of European football I have ever seen on an English football ground'. Bill Nicholson wistfully said he was disappointed Spurs had not won as he was confident his side would have beaten Real Madrid in the final and become the first British club to win the trophy. Tottenham fans will never know, but in the list of glorious failures this near mythical game ranks among the greatest.

What was said after the game:

"We were no longer the innocents abroad." **Jimmy Greaves**

"Tottenham fought very well. The half line is one of the best I ever played against in the world. Mackay is an extraordinary player." **Coluna**, Benfica's inside left

"Tottenham are one of the best teams in Europe. This was the hardest game we have ever played." **Pereira**, Benfica's goalkeeper

Some numbers from the 1961/62 European Cup run:

£80,000: total Spurs earned from the eight European Cup ties.
£200: total bonuses the players earned in the cup run.
508,087: total attendance at Spurs' ties.
244,087: total attendance at the four legs at White Hart Lane.

— RESULTS TO REMEMBER —

Tottenham's Top 10 most emphatic victories:

Result	Competition	Date
13–2 v Crewe Alexandra	FA Cup 4th round replay	February 3rd 1960
9–0 v Bristol Rovers	Division Two	October 26th 1977
9–0 v Keflavik	UEFA Cup, 1st round	September, 28th 1971
9–0 v Worksop	FA Cup 3rd round	January 15th 1923
9–1 v Tranmere Rovers	FA Cup 3rd round	January 12th 1953
8–0 v Southampton	Division Two	March 28th 1936
8–0 v Drogheda	UEFA Cup, 1st Round	September 28th 1983
9–2 v Nottingham Forest	Division One	September 29th 1962
8–1 v Burnley	Division Two	September 1st 1930
8–1 v Gornik Zabrze	European Cup, prelim round	September 20th 1961

— RESULTS TO FORGET —

The 10 results Spurs fans don't like to talk about:

Result	Competition	Date
0–7 v Liverpool	Division One	September 2nd 1978
2–8 v Derby County	Division One	October 16th 1976
1–7 v Newcastle Utd	Premier League	December 28th 1996
0–6 v Sunderland	Division One	February 21st 1934
0–6 v Arsenal	Division One	March 6th 1935
0–6 v Leicester City	Division One	March 28th 1935
0–6 v Sheffield United	Premier League	March 2nd 1993
2–7 v Liverpool	Division One	October 31st 1914
2–7 v Newcastle	Division One	September 1st 1951
2–7 v Blackburn	Division One	September 7th 1963

— GERMAN BITE —

At a snow-covered White Hart Lane on January 8th 1901, Spurs beat a German Football Association select team 9–6.

— HE'S ONE OF US —

Steve Perryman is hugely popular with Tottenham supporters not simply for his application on the pitch and long record of service to the club – he's garnered a cult following for his approach to non-football matters.

In 1970, he ran out on the pitch sporting a suedehead – a fashionable, cropped hairstyle – the first time teenage fans had seen anyone who shared their taste in fashion turn out for the Lilywhites.

And in Hunter Davies's classic 1972 book *The Glory Game*, Perryman's responses to the author's questions on social attitudes also made him stand apart. Asked for his political leanings, he said: "Labour. Definitely. Aren't all the players Labour?" Most were in fact Tory voters or not interested. But, as Davies revealed in his notes, Perryman had strong views, particularly on tax, saying: "It's got to be paid."

— FLESH AND BLOOD —

After picking up an eye injury in January 1983, midfielder Mickey Hazard was the grateful recipient of a year's supply of free steak from Robertson Butcher's in Hoddesdon. Hazard was pictured in the club programme applying a slab of steak to his eye, alongside Ricky Villa. Villa was also sponsored by Robertson's, presumably because, as an Argentinean he no doubt loved his beef. (In retirement, Villa became an owner of a cattle ranch).

— CHEERS! —

When new striker Dimitar Berbatov remarked that he was sad Spurs fans had not come up with a song for him, fansites and *The Sun* newspaper began the search for a suitable ditty. A few were tried, but none bettered this effort, sung to the tune of *Jesus Christ, Superstar*.

Dimitar
Berbatov
When he scores goals we say mazeltov!

— THE PEOPLES GAME —

A rundown of record Spurs attendances:

HIGHS
Record attendance: 114,815
FA Cup final, April 20th 1901 (at Crystal Palace)

Record attendance at White Hart Lane: 75,038
v Sunderland, FA Cup 6th round, March 5th 1938

Highest league attendance at WHL: 70,882
v Manchester United, Division One, September 21st 1951

Highest League Cup attendance at WHL: 55,923
v Arsenal, semi-final 2nd leg, December 4th 1968

Highest European home attendance: 64,448
v Benfica, European Cup semi-final 2nd leg, April 5th 1962

Highest European away attendance: 95,000
v Real Madrid, UEFA Cup semi-final, March 20th 1985

Highest post-war average attendance at WHL (league): 55,509
Division One, 1950/51

LOWS
Lowest attendance at WHL: 500
v Bristol Rovers, Western League on September 9th 1907 (Spurs won 10–0!)

Lowest league attendance at WHL: 5,000
v Sunderland, Division One, December 19th 1914

Lowest FA Cup attendance at WHL: 11,600
v Reading, quarter-final, March 28th 1901

Lowest League Cup attendance at WHL: 12,299
v Barnsley, 2nd round, October 8th 1986

Lowest European attendance at WHL: 18,105
v Grasshopper Zurich, UEFA Cup 1st round, October 3rd 1973

— THE HAIR NECESSITIES —

Former centre half Neil Ruddock changed his name by deed poll in May 2006 to become 'Wax Ruddock', as part of a sponsorship deal with a hair-removal product from Veet. Ruddock was officially known as 'Wax' for the duration of the 2006 World Cup, and to display the effectiveness of the product he had his chest hair removed so as to make an image of the Cross of St George.

— NICE GUY, CYRIL —

Such was the popularity of attacking full back Cyril Knowles that a star-studded line-up turned out for his memorial match in 1991. Cyril died on August 31st 1991, aged only 47. On November 10th, Remembrance Sunday, White Hart Lane staged two memorial games. The first, a short contest between Spurs and Arsenal 1970/71 which finished 0–0, was started by boxer Frank Bruno and featured the following line-ups:

Spurs: Pat Jennings, Joe Kinnear, Steve Perryman, John Pratt, Mike England, Phil Beal, Phil Holder, Greame Souness, Martin Peters, Martin Chivers, Alan Gilzean, Jimmy Neighbour, Ralph Coates, Peter Taylor.

Arsenal: Paul Barron, Sammy Nelson, Frank McClintock, Willie Young, Peter Storey, George Graham, Alan Ball, David Price, David Court, Liam Brady, George Armstrong, Jon Sammels, John Radford, Charlie George.

The main attraction was Spurs 1981/82 v Spurs 1990/91, which featured the following teams, finished 2–2.

Spurs 1981/82: Ray Clemence, Chris Hughton, Paul Miller, Graham Roberts, Glenn Hoddle, Ossie Ardiles, Micky Hazard, Ricky Villa, Garth Crooks, Steve Archibald, Mark Falco, Tony Galvin.

Spurs 1990/91: Erik Thorstvedt, Kevin Deardon, Ian Hendon, Justin Edinburgh, Steve Sedgley, David Howells, Nayim, David Tuttle, Gudni Bergsson, Vinny Samways, Peter Garland, John Hendry, Paul Walsh, Matthew Edwards, Paul Allen, Scott Houghton.

In the event programme, Memorial Committee organiser Morris Keston said: "Not a single player who was approached to mark this sad occasion turned down the invitation to appear. We could have fielded eight teams, let alone four."

— GLORIOUS NOTHING —

The 1986/87 season was a bittersweet one for Tottenham fans. Spurs once again lit up the football world with innovative, flowing football, but in the end, despite challenging on three fronts, finished with nothing.

It was manager David Pleat's first season in charge. After six wins in the first 15 games, Pleat changed the Spurs formation from 4-4-2 to a 4-5-1 that was inspired by Michel Platini's 1984 French side and the Belgian national side of 1986. The new tactics were first aired at Oxford on November 22nd, Spurs winning 4–2 and gaining rave reviews. In the next 19 matches Spurs lost only four times.

The system relied on a mobile five-man midfield – usually Paul Allen, Glenn Hoddle, Ossie Ardiles, Tony Galvin and Steve Hodge – supporting goal poacher supreme Clive Allen in the lone striker's role. Allen scored 49 goals in all competitions. In one patch, Spurs won five games on the trot, scoring 12 and conceding none.

The highlight came with a stunning display of skill and power at White Hart Lane in the League Cup quarter-final replay, with Spurs beating West Ham 5–0. But a fixture pile-up caused by weather postponements and cup replays eventually did for Spurs. Faced with 14 league and cup games in five weeks, Spurs fell away from Liverpool and eventual champions Everton in the league. In the League Cup, a titanic two-legged semi-final went to a replay and third game before Arsenal knocked them out – a result that was even harder to take as the Gunners had led for only one minute in five hours of football. Three days later, popular defender Danny Thomas had his career ended after a shocking tackle by QPR's Gavin McGuire.

Spurs did make the FA Cup final, and were hot favourites to beat Coventry, but the Sky Blues famously won a pulsating game thanks to Gary Mabbutt's knee, a deflected shot off the Spurs defender giving the Midlanders the winner. It was the first FA Cup final Spurs had lost, prompting a furious row between captain Richard Gough and Pleat at the post-match dinner.

Only Clive Allen collected any silverware, winning both the PFA and Football Writers' Association 'Footballer of the Year' awards.

— NO DELIGHT AT ANGELS —

In 1963, Conservative Home Secretary Henry Brooke was asked to invoke the blasphemy laws against Spurs after the team paraded the European Cup-Winners Cup through the streets of Tottenham on the Sunday after the win.

Reverend Clifford Hill of the High Cross Congregational Church took exception to three fans who, taking their inspiration from the club's anthem *Glory Glory Hallelujah*, dressed as angels and walked alongside the team bus carrying placards with the slogans 'Hallowed be thy names' and 'Adore them, for they are glorious'. His telegraph to the Home Secretary read:

This is an outrage to Christians. I am publicly warning the Spurs that if their supporters carry similar banners in future I shall do everything in my power to stop it. The idolisation of a football team by taking quotations from the Bible is wrong and offends Christians.

Perhaps conscious that the vicar could well call on his gaffer to use everything in his power too, the fans concerned – Peter Kirby, 31, Dave Casey, 27 and Mike Curly, 24 – decided on a dignified retreat.

"It's back to civvies for us," said Kirby. "We have apologised to people who feel offended. We have been appearing for two seasons and against the few who object there are thousands who have welcomed our little performances without taking them in a way in which they were never intended."

The fans had originally turned up in their heavenly garb after Tottenham's first game in Europe away against Polish side Gornik Zabrze (See *Angelic Upstarts*, page 35). Tottenham's physical approach had resulted in accusations from the Poles that the Spurs team so revered in England for their silky skills were 'no angels'. In the home leg, Kirby and his pals paraded around the edge of the pitch with their costumes and banners.

— NICE ONE CYRIL —

Forget Bowie, Slade and glam rock, it was a tribute to Cyril Knowles that rang through the charts in 1973. The classic single 'Nice One Cyril' by the Cockerel Chorus was released on the Youngblood label in February 1973, a few weeks before the League Cup Final between Spurs and Norwich City. The catchy tune reached a chart high of number 14 and stayed in the Top 50 for 12 weeks.

— REAL BAD LUCK —

Tottenham Hotspur were unbeaten at home in a European tie for 44 games over 24 years until March 6th 1985 when they lost 1–0 to Real Madrid in the UEFA Cup quarter-final at White Hart Lane.

This was also the first time Spurs had failed to score in a home European tie. To complete a miserable night, the goal came via a ricochet off the knee of captain Steve Perryman. Perryman's luck was out for the whole tie, as he was sent off in the 79th minute of the second leg at the Bernabeu as his team crashed out of the competition, managing only a 0–0 draw, after Mark Falco's perfectly good goal was disallowed for offside.

— WHEN CRUYFF MET HODDLE —

On October 19th 1983 two of the greatest players of the modern age faced each other in the second round of the UEFA Cup at White Hart Lane. For the visitors, Feyenoord, the Dutch master Johann Cruyff was bidding for a final peak in a glorious career. But for Tottenham Hotspur, Glenn Hoddle was about to show there was a new master at work.

The battle of the two number 10s had been eagerly anticipated, especially by Cruyff who later said, "I wanted to test myself against the young star of the present." In fact, it was to be Cruyff's obsession with the Englishman that cost his team the tie. As technical director and player it fell to Cruyff to decide tactics and, against the advice of Feyenoord boss Thijs Libreghts, he decided to mark Hoddle. For 20 minutes, Hoddle tortured the Dutchman, turning him inside out before Cruyff reorganised the team. But Hoddle by then had already tilted the tie irrevocably in Tottenham's direction with a master class in passing and crossing.

On eight minutes, a through ball to Chris Hughton enabled the full-back to cross for Steve Archibald to open the scoring. On 18 minutes, a perfect Hoddle cross was headed home by Tony Galvin. Five minutes later Archibald took advantage of another defence-splitting ball from Hoddle to make it 3–0. Then, six minutes before half-time an audacious 40-yard pass from Hoddle enabled Galvin to run through a by-now bewitched defence to tuck simply away. Spurs won the match 4–2, then outclassed the Dutch side in Rotterdam in the return, winning 2–0.

Cruyff admitted his decision was "a bad error of judgement". He said of Hoddle: "I thought I could mark him and keep him quiet. The result shows that I could not. He was a player that I had liked but it was only on the pitch that I realised how good he was. I was a shadow without any presence."

— EUROPEAN ROLL-CALL —

By the conclusion of the 2006/07 campaign, Spurs had played 52 different clubs since they first entered European competition in 1962. Feyenoord are the opponents Spurs have played most often, with the two clubs having been drawn together no fewer than five times. However, the teams have only actually played each other four times as the Rotterdam club were expelled from the competition in 2006/07 following crowd trouble involving their fans, and Spurs were given a bye.

Hadjuk Split (three times) Bayern Munich, Sporting Braga and FC Bruges (all twice) are the only other sides Spurs have faced on more than one occasion in Europe. The full list of opponents is . . .

Aberdeen, AC Milan, Ajax, Anderlecht, UT Arad, Atletico Madrid, Austria Vienna, Barcelona, Bayern Munich (2), OFK Belgrade, Benfica, Besiktas, Bohemians Prague, FC Bruges (2), Dinamo Bucharest, Coleraine, FC Cologne, Dinamo Tbilisi, Dukla Prague, Drogheda United, Dundalk, Eintracht Frankfurt, Feyenoord (5), Glasgow Rangers, Gornik Zabre, Grasshopper Club Zurich, Hadjuk Split (3), Keflavik, FC Kaiserslautern, Bayer Leverkusen, Liverpool, Lokomotive Leipzig, Luzern, Lyn Oslo, Manchester United, Nantes, Olympique Lyonnais, Olympiakos Piraeus, Osters IF (Vaxjo), Slavia Prague, FC Porto, Rapid Bucharest, Real Madrid, Red Star Belgrade, Rudar Velenje, Sevilla, Slovan Bratislava, Sparkasse Stockerau, Sporting Braga (2), Vitoria Setubal, Wolverhampton Wanderers, FC Zimbru.

— THE BEST TOTTENHAM JEWISH JOKE . . . EVER —

Much has traditionally been made of Tottenham Hotspur's connection with the Jewish community, whose humour has infused the Spurs-supporting experience for years. In the totally unscientific opinion of the authors, this is the pick of the crop. The authors' thanks go to the inspirational members of the Anjou Luncheon Club for this classic.

> *Two Jewish Spurs fans, Manny and Ted, meet in the street one summer's day. Says Manny, who is a little agitated: 'Have you seen the fixture list?'*
> *Ted: 'No, what's the problem?'*
> *Manny: 'It's the Spurs v Arsenal game, it's on the same day as Yom Kippur!'*
> *Ted: 'Really. That's not good. What are we going to do?'*
> *Manny: 'We'll have to record it'.*
> *Ted: 'What, the whole service?'*

— SPURS LEGENDS: PAT JENNINGS —

The only player who could bring Spurs and Arsenal fans together in their appreciation, Pat Jennings is a legend. Tall and blessed with enormous hands, the Northern Ireland-born keeper won medals with both clubs and is the only player to have been given a testimonial by both Spurs and the other lot.

Jennings began his career with Newry Town prior to joining Watford for £6,000 in May 1963. A year later Bill Nicholson snapped him up for £27,000, a fee which turned out to be an absolute bargain. A former Gaelic footballer, Big Pat controlled his area and marshalled his defence with a quiet confidence. He was a superb shot-stopper who stood out in one-on-ones, and in 1967 even scored a goal via a mighty clearance in the 3–3 Charity Shield draw against Manchester United (See *Big Pat's Big Kick*, page 129). He won the FA Cup (1967), League Cup (1971 and 1973) and UEFA Cup (1972) with Spurs, and was named 'Footballer of the Year' in 1972/73 and PFA 'Footballer of the Year' in 1975/76. In 1976, the year of his testimonial against Arsenal, Pat was awarded the MBE. Pat also took ownership of the green jersey for Northern Ireland, making a then world record 119 international appearances throughout his career.

When Spurs were relegated in 1977, Keith Burkinshaw allowed Jennings to leave after 591 competitive appearances for the club. It is a mistake Burkinshaw has always admitted to, as Jennings went on to excel for Arsenal for a further eight seasons, winning one FA Cup winners medal, although even Pat's skills weren't enough to prevent him losing a further two FA Cup finals and a Cup Winners Cup final with the Gunners. In 1985, Arsenal gave Pat a testimonial against the only possible opponents – Tottenham Hotspur.

He returned to White Hart Lane as goalkeeping cover later the same year, and played for his country in the 1986 World Cup finals before announcing his retirement. He made one more appearance in a Spurs shirt, on the January 10th 1986 in the Screensport Super Cup, Spurs losing 2–0 at home to Liverpool.

Today his association with the club continues – at the time of writing he is one of Tottenham's goalkeeping coaches.

— SPURS EXPRESS —

In common with several football clubs, Tottenham have had train engines named in the side's honour. LNER Locomotive 2830, formerly 'Thoresby Park', took the name 'Tottenham Hotspur' and plied lines across North London until it was withdrawn from service in 1958.

— THIS ISN'T YOUR LIFE —

In the early sixties, ITV's *This Is Your Life* was one of the most-watched shows on British TV. Every week viewers would tune in eagerly to see who host Eamonn Andrews would step out of the shadows to brandish his trademark red book at and announce in dulcet tones "This is your life". The tension was even more pronounced because the surprise was filmed live. At least, it was until the show targeted Danny Blanchflower in 1961, when the following scene unfolded . . .

Eamonn Andrews, stepping out of the shadows: "Danny Blanchflower, This Is Your Life."
Blanchflower, angrily brushing the mic away. "No it isn't!"
[Cue confusion and commercial break.]

A repeat of an earlier show was hastily run, and that was the last time the show was filmed live. Blanchflower, a man who guarded his privacy fiercely, was angry and embarrassed at what he saw as an intrusion. But Bill Nicholson, one of many friends and colleagues who had gathered in the studio to await the subject of the show, was furious with Danny. He turned to Cliff Jones and said, "Jesus Christ. Trust him. Trust him to do it. I've wasted a day's work coming up here!"

— BECAUSE I'M WORTH IT —

After an impressive international display for Wales against Brazil, Cliff Jones was hailed by some among the press as 'the best winger in the world'. Reasoning he was therefore due a pay rise, after training he told his team-mates he was going into Bill Nicholson's office to demand an increase. His colleagues decided to wait in the White Hart pub for the outcome. Minutes later, Jones walked in.

"I went into his office," said Jones, "and came straight out with it. I said, 'Bill, I want £100 a week. Everybody thinks I'm the best winger in the world.' Without looking up Bill said, 'Do they? I don't. Now eff off.'"

— GET WITH THE PROGRAME —

In a sign of times long past, the introduction to the Spurs v Chelsea 1967 FA Cup Final programme – price one shilling – featured the following pledge from the publishers. "The publishers of this Wembley souvenir have made a sincere and serious effort to give you factual and informative details about the men who make Tottenham and Chelsea tick."

— ORIGINAL RIVALS —

Tottenham Hotspur's original local rivals were an Edmonton-based schools side, Latymer. The fixture against Latymer is described in *The Official Illustrated History of Tottenham Hotspur* (Hamlyn, 1995) as 'the Spurs v Arsenal clash of its day'.

There was much local interest in the fixture, and plenty of controversy. Latymer arrived for the match on December 27th 1883 with only five players, although two arrived later. Somehow the game went ahead but when it finished the two sides could not agree on the score. Hotspur, as Spurs were called at the time, said it was 2–0 to them but the result remained unprinted in the local paper, the *Tottenham Weekly Herald*. The *Herald* did remark, however, that the Hotspur fans had dished out much verbal abuse to the followers of their rivals.

Things got worse in the next fixture, with a clearly peeved *Herald* reporting that, as the club captains had sent in contradictory reports of the game, the paper would not print anything else about the clubs until they resolved their dispute.

The following season Latymer cheekily fielded 12 men until the scam was discovered at half-time. Despite this ruse, Hotspur still ran out 2–0 winners. When the Edmonton club attempted the same thing in a reserve fixture the following season, Hotspur dropped the fixture due to 'ungentlemanly conduct' and the first great North London derby was pronounced dead.

Almost a century later, the official history of Latymer School gave an interesting insight into how the early 'Hotspurs' were perceived: "Despite their Presbyterian background, they seem to have been from the start a boisterous group. They were expelled from their HQ in the YMCA for kicking a ball up a chimney. A number of other charges laid against them included playing cards and stealing mulberries. They joined a CoE Young Men's Society on condition they attended church on Sundays but were caught playing cards in the pews." And this from a team that twice tried to field 12 men!

— BUM NOTE —

Gary Mabbutt was and is a hero to Spurs fans, but only once received the compliment afforded him by supporter Carol Jenkins of Woodford Green in the match programme for the visit of Liverpool on November 4th 1990.

Carol's verdict? "He's got the best bum in Britain."

— VICTORIAN VALUES —

In the official club handbook for 1897, the following 'Hints to Spectators' were listed.

Learn the rules well before criticising.

Respect the rulings of the referee and refrain from unseemly demonstrations so common on many football fields when decisions are unpalatable – the best of referees make mistakes.

Applaud good football impartially.

Don't let a defeat discourage you. It is at this time that encouragement is most wanted by players.

Don't express your disapproval of a player so that everyone can hear, it only upsets him and he loses confidence.

This season's team will doubtless accomplish some fine performances. Don't, in your enthusiasm, forget that there is such a thing as mistaken kindness where athletes in training are concerned.

Don't stop at home when the team goes away; they want your support more than ever when on opponents' grounds.

Let visitors go away with the impression that the Tottenham crowd are good sportsmen.

Whether at home or away don't forget the 'Tottenham whisper'
[No, we don't know what the Tottenham whisper is either.]

— NEIGHBOURS FROM HELL —

Arsenal v Tottenham is like no other derby match in any of the great soccer centres of Britain. It is not based on the sectarian divisions of Glasgow; it lacks the bitter jealousy of Manchester City's attempts to catch up with United; there is none of the internecine strife which splits families on Merseyside. It is more like neighbours who detest one another so much, for reasons long forgotten, that getting one up on the other lot makes a fan's day.
Legendary sports writer Frank McGhee in *The Observer* just before the 1995/96 derby at White Hart Lane, which Spurs won 2–1, thanks to goals from Teddy Sheringham and Chris Armstrong.

— FLYING HIGH —

When Spurs flew to the European Cup Winners' Cup Final in Rotterdam in May 1963, the crew of the chartered Viscount plane that carried them there had a few Spurs connections themselves.

Co-pilot Chick Evans was a season ticket holder who had been following the team since he played truant to see them in 1936. Flight Steward Jack Gott was founder of the BEA Stewards Xl, who were dubbed 'the Spurs of London Airport' because of their success. The rest of the crew, which had accompanied Bill Nicholson's men throughout the campaign, comprised Captain Doug Evans, Senior Steward Tony Kernighan, and Stewardess Sylvia Swanepoel, who told the *Daily Mirror*, "The players are wonderfully behaved, but very hard to relax. The only trouble I have is trying to break up the card games to serve the meals."

Although the crew missed the final because duty called, they had all been guests of the club for every home tie in the cup run.

— SPURS LEGENDS: GARY LINEKER —

Second only to Jimmy Greaves as the most lethal natural finisher ever to play for Spurs, Lineker's strike-rate of 80 goals in 139 appearances for the club speaks for itself. When he signed for Tottenham in June 1989 for £1.2 million he was already established as a world-class striker, his reputation honed at the great Everton team of the mid-80s and with Spanish giants Barcelona.

For England, Lineker's combination with Peter Beardsley was also deadly, and he remains his country's second highest goalscorer of all time, with 48 goals in 80 games, one behind Bobby Charlton.

The most frequent criticism of Lineker was that 'all he does is score goals', and he was the first to admit he hated training and grafting. But he did his job better than anyone. His pace allowed him to play off the shoulder of the last defender, while his positional sense meant he was always in the right place to tap home in the box. He scored few great goals, but was a great scorer of goals. He was also a model professional, his record of never receiving a booking making him a real-life Roy of the Rovers.

He left Spurs in 1992 to join Nagoya Grampus Eight in Japan's fledgling J-League.

— WHITE HART LANE 3:
THE PAXTON AND PARK LANE —

The stands behind each goal at White Hart Lane are officially described as the plain North and South Stands but are known to Spurs fans as 'the Paxton' and 'the Park Lane'.

Both ends were plain terraces in the stadium's early days, with the Paxton known as the 'Edmonton Goal'. Between 1921 and 1923, each terrace was roofed according to the standard Archibald Leitch blueprint. The distinguishing feature of both stands was how their roofs drifted away from the touchline, following the street plan of Paxton Road and Park Lane.

That was how they remained with only minor alterations. Seats were installed for 3,000 fans in each upper section in the early 1960s, while in 1972 a section of the terracing was chopped out behind the Park Lane goal to prevent missiles being thrown at the opposition goalkeeper.

During the wholesale redevelopment of White Hart Lane, given added impetus by the Taylor Reports of 1989 that led to the enforcement of all-seater stadiums at top-flight grounds, the Paxton and Park Lane had to wait for their turns after the West and East Stand building work. After seats were installed on the remaining terrace sections, a new roof was assembled over the Paxton end using the 'goalpost' design that suspended the structure beneath a steel frame. At a cumulative cost of £16m, the Park Lane was completely rebuilt and a new upper tier added to the Paxton. As a flourish, Jumbotron TV screens were installed in each roof, giving White Hart Lane the look of a 'mini Bernabeu'.

A feature of White Hart Lane is that the ground has never had a 'home end' in the same way that Anfield and Old Trafford have, but the Paxton and the Park Lane have both provided committed encouragement for the team down the years, particularly the Park Lane. With the changes made to the East Stand and the loss of the Shelf, this is now home to the bulk of Tottenham's singing support.

The Paxton holds 10,086, just 600 fewer than the East Stand, the Park Lane 8,573, contributing to a total ground capacity of 36,241.

— THE FANS' DERBY —

The biggest north London derby crowds . . .

Biggest home crowd: 69,821 on October 10th 1953 (White Hart Lane)
Biggest away crowd: 72,164 on September 29th 1951 (Highbury)
Biggest ever crowd: 77,893 on April 14th 1991 (FA Cup semi-final at Wembley)

— JENAS BABIES —

Before every game, Spurs and England midfielder Jermaine Jenas eats five Jelly Babies.

"For the sugar rush I suppose. And they're nice," he told women's glossy magazine *Marie Claire* in June 2006.

Jenas also revealed that "after training, I love Jaffa Cakes", proving that nutritional habits have come a long way since Messrs Greaves and Venables used to pop out to the Corner Pin for a half-time pint.

— CLASSIC MATCHES 5: ST HOTSPUR'S DAY —

Spurs 3   **Arsenal 1**
Lineker (2)   Smith
Gascoigne

April 14th 1991: FA Cup semi-final
Wembley
Att: 77,893

One of the most extraordinary derbies ever was played on April 14th 1991 when Spurs were drawn against their old rivals in the semi-final of the FA Cup. Such was the demand for tickets that the FA allowed Wembley to be used for a semi-final for the first time, and the 77,893 crowd proved how wise that decision was.

Arsenal were red-hot favourites, top of the table with just one league defeat all season. Spurs, on the other hand, had only won twice in the league since Christmas and were a club embroiled in boardroom wrangles and threatened with financial crisis. Their cup run had been inspired by Paul Gascoigne, who had almost single-handedly dragged them through. But Gascoigne had had an operation on a long-standing stomach injury and had only played an hour of football since going under the knife. His return to the first team had led to him being dubbed 'the abdominal showman'.

Spurs fans feared the worst, but within nine minutes they were in dreamland. Anders Limpar brought Paul Stewart down 30 yards out after five minutes. Gascoigne stepped up to take the free-kick and sent an incredible strike around the two-man wall and into the top corner. The Spurs sections erupted at what was one of the old stadium's finest ever goals. Four minutes later Spurs were 2–0 up when Gary Lineker tapped in from close range.

Spurs were in total control, playing a slick, short-passing game in which a Vinny Samways inspired five-man midfield taunted their opponents before releasing Lineker to punch holes in the Arsenal defence. Then, just before half-time and against the run of play, Alan Smith scored to give Arsenal hope. Spurs looked to be in for a tough second half.

But it was Tottenham's defence which proved its worth, snuffing out Arsenal's efforts to level the game. Gascoigne went off on the hour to wild applause, making way for Nayim. Almost immediately, Tottenham went on the attack. Gary Mabbutt won the ball and released Lineker, Samways drew the defence, and Lineker slotted home to make it 3–1.

Spurs had won in the sweetest way possible. They had played great football, spiked their fiercest rivals' Double ambitions, and very probably secured the future existence of Tottenham Hotspur itself. And Gascoigne's goal ensured that St Hotspur's Day would live long in the memory.

"Wahey the Spurs"

— SHALL WE SING A SONG FOR YOU? —

Despite the many fine FA Cup final singles issued by Spurs squads over the years, the number one spot in the pop charts has always been occupied by someone else on the day of the big match. Since the modern charts began, the full list of Spurs cup final No1s is:

Year	Title	Artist
1961	*Blue Moon*	The Marcels
1962	*Wonderland*	The Shadows
1967	*Silence is Golden*	The Tremeloes
1981	*Stand and Deliver*	Adam and the Ants
1982	*A Little Peace*	Nicole
1987	*Nothing's Gonna Stop Us Now*	Starship
1991	*The Shoop Shoop Song (It's In His Kiss)*	Cher

— THE OTHER CUP —

Spurs have won the League Cup three times, most recently in 1999 when Allan Nielsen scored a last-minute winner against Leicester City at Wembley.

In the competition as a whole Spurs have played 176 games, winning 105, drawing 29 and losing 42. The goal difference is pretty healthy, too, showing 341 goals scored to 183 conceded. The club's biggest victory came on December 3rd 1975, when Doncaster Rovers suffered a 7–2 thrashing.

When Spurs lost the 1982 League Cup final 3–1 to Liverpool it was the first domestic cup final the club had ever lost, and the first reverse at Wembley. The 2–1 defeat to Blackburn Rovers in the 2002 final was at Cardiff in the club's only appearance to date at the Millennium Stadium. The club's winning League Cup appearances are:

Year	Venue	Result	Scorers
1971	Wembley	Tottenham 2 Aston Villa 0	Chivers 2
1973	Wembley	Tottenham 1 Norwich City 0	Coates
1999	Wembley	Tottenham 1 Leicester City 0	Nielsen

— CUP FINAL DAY OUT —

Much has been written about the 100th FA Cup Final in 1981, still regarded as possibly the best ever. For those completists who want a full record of the day, this was the 'Timetable and Programme of Events' for the big day.

1.10pm–1.35pm Selections by the massed bands of the Royal Marines, under the direction of Lt Col J R Mason, principal director of music, Royal Marines.

1.35pm–2pm Display by the Wonderwings.

2–2.10pm Pitch inspection and walkabout by the two Cup Final teams.

2.10–2.30pm Introduction of captains of past winning finalists.

2.30–2.45pm Music by the massed bands of the Royal Marines.

2.45pm Singing of the traditional Cup Final hymn Abide With Me. Accompanied by the Derek Taverner Singers.

2.50pm The National Anthem. Presentation of the teams to her Majesty the Queen Mother.

3pm Kick-off

3.45pm Half-time. Marching display by the massed bands of the Royal Marines.

4.40pm End of match. Presentation of the FA Cup and medals by Her Majesty Queen Elizabeth the Queen Mother.

— THE MOTHER OF ALL DERBIES —

A magnificent-seven collection of memorable victories over the old enemy.

Spurs 2 Arsenal 1
White Hart Lane, November 7th 1999
Premier League
A result which proved the old adage that average teams raise their game for the big derby occasion. Spurs raced into a 2–0 lead after 19 minutes thanks to a poacher's finish from Steffen Iversen and Tim Sherwood's gobsmacking free kick. The Gunners responded as only they know how – pulling one back via Patrick Vieira and going down to nine men after both Freddie Ljungberg and Martin Keown were sent off.

Spurs 3 Arsenal 1
Wembley, April 14th 1991
FA Cup semi-final
Not only did Spurs prevent Arsenal from lifting the double, by reaching Wembley they arguably saved the debt-ridden club from going out of business. Five minutes in and from 35 yards, Paul Gascoigne prepared to take a free-kick. "Is Gascoigne going to have a crack?" pondered commentator Barry Davies. "He is, you know." Henceforth, Spurs supporters have renamed April 14th 'St Hotspur's Day' (See *Classic Matches 5*, page 119).

Arsenal 1 Spurs 2
Highbury, Jan 1st 1985
Division One
Spurs went top of the league thanks to goals from Garth Crooks and Mark Falco on the traditional derby date of New Year's Day (fans of a certain vintage will recall the then relatively common sight of tired and emotional supporters arriving for the 11.30am kick-off straight from the previous night's party, many in fancy dress). Graham Roberts charmed the home fans with a V-salute to Highbury's West Stand after the winner. A year later, Roberts propelled Arsenal's then great hope, 'Champagne' Charlie Nicholas, into Highbury's East Stand with a crunching tackle.

Spurs 5, Arsenal 0
White Hart Lane, April 4th 1983
Division One
Goals from Chris Hughton (2), Alan Brazil and Mark Falco (2) sent White Hart Lane delirious with joy. Falco's best goal – a shoulder high, 20-yard volley on the run – was one of the finest ever in the fixture. After the game, Spurs fans bade a fond farewell to the Arsenal team coach, singing 'Five nil, Five nil.' Legend has it that Pat Jennings, who had been dropped by Arsenal for the game and was sitting at the back of the bus, smiled and discreetly raised five fingers.

Spurs 4, Arsenal 3
White Hart Lane, August 26th 1961
Division One
Fresh from winning the Double, Spurs confirmed their North London dominance with a Terry Dyson hat-trick, the only man to hit three goals for Spurs in a North London (league) derby.

Arsenal 1, Spurs 3
Highbury, January 31st 1934
Division One
Arsenal were on their way to grinding out a second successive championship (part of a hat-trick of titles) but a resounding win at Highbury earned Spurs some temporary local bragging rights and ended the Gunners' unbeaten home record. The goals were scored by Willie Evans (2) and Les Howe.

Spurs 3, Woolwich Arsenal 1
White Hart Lane, December 3rd 1910
Division One
The first ever league victory for Spurs against Arsenal at the third attempt (after one defeat and one draw). Goals from Darnell, Minter and Humphreys put the south Londoners in their place.

— THOSE WHO SERVE —

It's not just the players and famous managers who make a football club what it is. Here are just a couple of the more unsung figures who became part of the White Hart Lane fabric:

Charles Roberts
Continuity was the name of the game for Tottenham once the club was established as a limited company in 1898. Charles Roberts became chairman in that year and remained in the seat until his death in 1943. He was a colourful character, organising various fund-raising events and extravaganzas and was a former pitcher for the Brooklyn Dodgers baseball team in New York.

Johnny Wallis, MBE
Legendary trainer and kit man, Wallis was one of the stars among the cast of minor players in Hunter Davies's classic book *The Glory Game,* an insider account of a season at Spurs in the 1970s.

Asked by Davies whether he provided the shampoo and deodorant for the players in the dressing room that was on offer at other clubs, Wallis replied: "Get out. They're supposed to be footballers, not bloody poofs. The only beauty extras we lay on are those green square things in the bath. Carbolic. You can't beat it."

Johnny's association with the club lasted from 1936 to 1994, initially as a reserve team player then as 'A' team manager, ending with a spell on the ground staff before retirement.

— THE GENERATION GAME —

Among the crowd for the 0–0 home draw against Aston Villa on January 22nd 2006 were Richard and Michael Mackman, who met skipper Ledley King after the game. This introduction meant that Richard and Michael had met both the most recent and the first-ever Spurs captain. They are the grandsons of Bobby Buckle, one of the 11 founding members of the club, later the joint secretary and the man who proposed the toast to celebrate winning the 1901 FA Cup at the post-match reception.

— THINK OF A NUMBER —

Ever wondered who was the bright spark that came up with the idea of shirt numbers? The game of football has Spurs to thank. Tottenham made repeated requests for the numbering system to be introduced by the Football League, before the idea was finally put into practice in 1939. The first time Spurs players wore numbered shirts was in January 1939, in an FA Cup tie against Watford.

— FIRST LEAGUE HAT-TRICK —

Billy Minter was the first Spurs player to score a hat-trick in a league game when he bagged three of the team's four goals in the 4–0 home win against Blackburn Rovers on March 28th 1910. Minter, an inside forward, was a prolific goalscorer during his time with the club, notching 151 goals in 334 matches between 1908 and 1926. He scored on his debut in a 2–1 home defeat by Millwall in 1908 and played in all but three of that season's campaign as Spurs secured promotion from the old Second Division. He topped the goalscoring charts in each of the following three seasons.

When the league resumed after the war, Minter was made club captain, retiring a year later to take over as trainer. In his first season in his new role, Spurs won the FA Cup. In 1927 he was made manager, but Spurs were relegated in his first season in charge and couldn't regain top-flight status. The stress this caused led to Minter retiring in 1929. He went on to be assistant secretary in 1932, a post he held until his death in 1940. He was a true Tottenham legend.

— LEAGUES APART —

In the 99 years since they joined the Football League, Spurs have played in the top flight for 73 out of a possible 88 seasons (the two World Wars suspended regular football for 11 seasons). The lowest position to which Tottenham have sunk was 12th place in Division Two in season 1929/30.

— WHISTLE STOP —

In the Easter Saturday home game against Manchester City in 1960, referee Gilbert Pullin awarded Spurs a penalty just before half-time. Though Cliff Jones's effort was saved by City goalkeeper Bert Trautmann, Jones buried the rebound, but to no avail: Pullin claimed he had blown the half time whistle as Trautmann saved the first shot. City went on to win 1–0.

— VIP VISITORS —

- Long before he found favour with Mrs Simpson, The Prince of Wales (later Edward VIII) dallied with an interest in football and paid a visit to Spurs in 1920.
- Prince Feisal, Governor of Mecca, saw Spurs beat West Brom 3–0 on September 25th 1926. The Prince said he was 'delighted with the game'.
- Then Prime Minister Clement Attlee was a guest for the 1–0 win over Charlton on December 30th 1950.
- Not known for her love of football, Hollywood superstar Jayne Mansfield visited White Hart Lane in 1960. Perched precariously on the edge of the Director's box above the West Stand paddock, Hollywood's blonde bombshell managed to keep her balance and her dignity as thousands of fans ignored the entertainment on the pitch to ogle the visual delights off it.
- Prime Minister Tony Blair paid a visit to White Hart Lane in April 2006 to meet Martin Jol, Chris Hughton, Ledley King and Paul Robinson as part of the launch of the Government and Premier League's 'Kickz' campaign that offers coaching to children from disadvantaged communities.
- The High Commissioner of Tanzania was a guest of the club to witness Spurs force 24 attempts on goal against Newcastle United in January 2007, yet still lose 3–2. Welcome to White Hart Lane, your excellency.

— SPURS LEGENDS: GRAHAM ROBERTS —

Compared with other Spurs' legends like Blanchflower, Jennings, Hoddle or Perryman, Graham Roberts played comparatively few games for the club – 276 between 1980 and 1986. Neither was he a football artist in the usual Tottenham tradition. But Roberts' commitment to the cause secured his place in Tottenham fans' hearts, evoking memories of Dave Mackay for many. He was a hard-tackling central midfielder/defender, but he was also one of the best passers of the ball seen in a Spurs shirt.

Signed in May 1980 from Weymouth, his fee of £35,000 was the highest ever paid for a non-league player. He'd been a schoolboy with home-town club Southampton before moving on to Bournemouth and Portsmouth as an amateur before breaking his ankle. He recovered and played part-time for Weymouth, working as a ship fitter's mate until Spurs signed him. A year later he was on the winning side in the 1981 Centenary Cup final, spitting out two broken teeth in the process to provide an iconic image of early-80s football. In the following year's final his long attacking run into QPR's box brought Spurs the penalty with which Glenn Hoddle won the replay.

Roberts' finest moment came in the second leg of the 1984 UEFA Cup final against Anderlecht. Roberts played out of his skin and dragged Spurs level six minutes from time, forcing the famous penalty shoot-out which Spurs won. He was still only 25 years old.

Roberts looked set for a long career at Spurs but in December 1986 he was transferred to Glasgow Rangers, a victim of David Pleat's managerial new broom.

— LOVE ON THE SHELF —

From the letters page of the club programme, Spurs v Bohemians of Prague, November 28th 1984:

During the Spurs v Liverpool Milk Cup game, I noticed this very nice girl that was standing on the Shelf. She had lightish coloured hair and was wearing a sheepskin coat with a Spurs scarf. I would really like to meet this girl. I was wearing a blue zip up denim jacket. My hair is brown and slightly spiked. To whoever you are, if you would like to meet me, stand in the same place for the Newcastle game. – yours Jim, Kent.

— EXPERT ANALYSIS —

A selection of former Spurs who have swapped shin pads and boots for TV or radio microphone. They include:

Gary Lineker
Paul Walsh
Chris Waddle
Garth Crooks
Clive Allen
Gary Stevens
Terry Venables
Jason Cundy
David Pleat
John Scales
Jimmy Greaves
Danny Blanchflower
Jamie Redknapp

— THE BEST OF THE BARD —

Harry Hotspur isn't the only Spurs legend with a Shakespeare connection. From Henry IV, Part 1, Act 1, Scene 1:

On Holy-rood day, the gallant Hotspur there
*Young Harry Percy, and brave **Archibald***
That ever valiant and approved Scot.'

— CLASSIC MATCHES 6: BRISTOL BUSTED —

Spurs 9   **Bristol Rovers 0**
Lee (4)
Moores (3)
Taylor
Hoddle

October 22nd 1977: Division Two
White Hart Lane
Att: 26,311

In the modern era, relegation from the top flight is viewed as the end of the world. In the mid-1970s, it was almost a relief. After a series of seasons in which they laboured to maintain their Division One status, Spurs finally succumbed in 1977, finishing bottom of the table.

The next campaign was Tottenham's first out of the top division for 27 years, but it gave a tired, listless club a much-needed opportunity to rebuild and revitalise itself.

Tottenham's brief second-flight sojourn provided many highlights (and some bumper 50,000+ crowds), but the best came with the home clash against Bristol Rovers. Spurs gave a debut to new striker Colin Lee, signed fresh from Torquay for £60,000. Before the game he was barely known to his new team-mates, but by the end he was a household name known to millions. Lee scored four as Keith Burkinshaw's side were allowed free reign to express themselves. Ian Moores chipped in with a hat trick while Peter Taylor and Glenn Hoddle completed the rout and Tottenham's best-ever league victory. Rovers' ex-Gunner Bobby Gould could only watch on and admire the exhibition.

— BIG PAT'S BIG KICK —

For the 1967 Charity Shield, Cup holders Spurs journeyed north to Old Trafford to meet league champions Manchester United in the traditional curtain raiser to the new season. Midway through the first half, Pat Jennings launched a huge drop kick from his own area. It sailed over the halfway line, cleared the United defence and looked to be heading powerfully but harmlessly into the arms of his opposite number, Alex Stepney.

Until, that is, the ball bounced, leaving a confused Stepney to misjudge its flight and scramble helplessly back as the ball flew over his head and into the net. Big Pat had scored, the first goalkeeper to do so direct from a goal kick for 67 years, emulating Manchester City's Charlie Williams who beat Sunderland's JE Doig on April 14th 1900. The 1967 game finished 3–3.

Pat's modern-day counterpart Paul Robinson repeated the feat with a remarkable goal in the home league game against Watford on March 17th 2007. Launching a free kick from just outside his own penalty area, Robinson notched the second goal of his career (he had struck for his previous club Leeds Utd.), as the ball bounced over Hornets' keeper Ben Foster and into the net.

— THE UNIVERSITY OF SPURS —

In 1950, Bill Nicholson was appointed as coach to the Cambridge University side. His opposite number at Oxford was Tottenham teammate Vic Buckingham.

— BOBBY'S BAGGY RECORD —

Bobby Smith just loved playing West Brom. Tottenham's second greatest top-scorer bagged 17 goals against the Baggies in 16 games – the most goals scored by any Spur player against an individual opposing team. Smith's tally included four in the 5–0 home win on April 18th 1959.

— MANILOW MAGIC —

It's one of the more unlikely terrace anthems, but The Carpenters' *Can't Smile Without You* – memorably given a new lease of life by Barry Manilow in 1978 – can still be heard at Spurs games today.

It's all because of a supporters' coach that runs from Palmers Green in North London. To ease the journey, tapes would be played over the coach PA, and *Can't Smile..* was always the last song on the tape as the coach pulled into home. The fans who used the coach took up the song, started singing it at away games and it caught on at home games. For the final game of the 2005/06 season, the team took to the pitch for their lap of honour with the classic ballad ringing in their ears.

— SPURS BEAT CHELSEA YET AGAIN —

Chelsea's 16-year unbeaten league reign against Spurs was finally ended when the north Londoners triumphed 2–1 in November 2006. Here's a selection of other memorable victories when Spurs have never felt more like singing the blues:

Result	Date	Competition
Spurs 4 Chelsea 1	September 4th 1985	Division 1
Chelsea 2 Spurs 3	March 6th 1982	FA Cup quarter-final
Spurs 2 Chelsea 0	April 19th 1975	Division 1
[this result effectively relegated Chelsea to Division Two]		
Spurs 2 Chelsea 1	May 20th 1967	FA Cup Final (at Wembley)
Spurs 5 Chelsea 2	December 30th 1961	Division 1
Spurs 4 Chelsea 0	September 3rd 1958	Division 1
Spurs 4 Chelsea 0	January 26th 1957	FA Cup 4th round
Spurs 4 Chelsea 0	February 25th 1956	Division 1
Chelsea 0 Spurs 4	September 30th 1933	Division 1
Chelsea 0 Spurs 4	October 16th 1920	Division 1
Spurs 5 Chelsea 0	October 9th 1920	Division 1

— SPURS LEGENDS: ARTHUR ROWE —

Arthur Rowe established the club as a force in the modern game. Born in Tottenham in 1906, he was a successful schoolboy footballer. He signed professional forms with the club in May 1929 and made his league debut in October 1931, quickly establishing himself as first-choice centre-half who exhibited a more constructive approach than many of his 'stopper' contemporaries.

Injuries severely restricted his appearances in 1933/34, a major factor in the club's relegation to the Second Division, and the club would not make it back to the top flight until Rowe's return as manager. In 1939, he was released from his contract after failing to recover from his cartilage problems. He went to Hungary to coach but shortly after his arrival war broke out and he returned to the UK, serving in the army as a physical training instructor and running the Army football team.

Demobbed in 1945, he became secretary-manager of Chelmsford City, winning the Southern League Cup in his first season and quickly establishing them as one of the country's top non-league sides. In 1949, Spurs offered him the manager's job, which he accepted eagerly to replace Joe Hume. Rowe's first signing was future-World Cup winning manager Alf Ramsey from Southampton, and the right-back was to be an essential part of Rowe's team which won promotion in his first season, and the club's first Football League title in the second.

A modest man, Rowe maintained that his tactical philosophy was simply an extension of the 'Spurs Way' – attractive, fast-paced football committed to attack. But, in a precursor of the style made famous by the Hungarian national side of the 1950s, Rowe revolutionised the concept of passing. He insisted his Spurs players pass the ball simply and quickly, instantly moving into space to take the return pass, creating a flowing, instinctive style that, in Rowe's words, gave a game an 'electric shock'.

This system was dubbed 'Push and run'. Rowe never liked the term, but given expression by quality players such as Ronnie Burgess, Len Duquemin, Les Bennett, Eddie Baily, Sonny Walters, Bill Nicholson and Ramsey it was thrillingly effective. Opponents were left only to scratch their heads and many a time after a game, Tottenham players were asked by bewildered and beaten foes: "How did you do that?"

It wasn't to last. The team soon aged and ill-health forced Rowe's retirement in 1955. But at heart, he remained a Tottenham purist. Filmed for the BBC's centenary special on Spurs in 1982, a frail Rowe was asked what Tottenham meant to him.

"I like them," he answered with massive understatement, his voice cracking with emotion, "and to be associated with them for all those years was nice."

— CLASSIC MATCHES 7: SOUTHAMPTON —

Southampton 2,	Spurs 6
Shipperley	Rosenthal (3)
Le Tissier	Sheringham
	Barmby

March 1st 1995: FA Cup 5th round replay
The Dell
Att.: 15,172

Two-nil down at half time and facing an ignominious exit from the FA Cup, Spurs found salvation in the unlikely guise of Ronny Rosenthal.

An Israeli international signed from Liverpool the previous year for £250,000, 'Rocket' Ronny was never the most accomplished of strikers but earned his place in White Hart Lane folklore by engineering an astonishing comeback. After Spurs had conceded two goals to Neil Shipperley and Matt Le Tissier, manager Gerry Francis sent on his secret weapon in the 35th minute, under orders to 'take the initiative'. By the end of the match, Rosenthal hadn't so much taken the initiative as seized it, throttled it and left it lying on the ground begging for mercy.

First he drilled home a Nick Barmby cross on 56 minutes; two minutes later, he went on a mazy dribble and unleashed a 25-yard thunderbolt to draw Spurs level and take the match into extra time; in the 101st minute another cracker left Saints keeper Bruce Grobbelaar with no chance and gave Spurs an unlikely lead. Further goals from Sheringham, Barmby and Anderton completed an incredible fight back – but the game undoubtedly belonged to hat trick hero Rocket Ronny.

— CHIVERS REGAL —

Martin Chivers holds the record as Tottenham's most prolific scorer in European competition, with 22 goals, all in the UEFA Cup.

— THE TEAM NOW LEAVING FROM PLATFORM 13 . . . —

Legend has it that when Crewe Alexandra arrived for their record 13–2 thrashing against Spurs in the FA Cup on February 4th 1960, their train terminated at Euston Station's platform 2. Travelling back home, they set off from, yep you guessed it, platform 13!

— NO BUSINESS LIKE SHOWBUSINESS —

Arsenal used to have the Metropolitan Police Band providing half time 'entertainment' at Highbury, greeted every season by the chant of 'Hello, hello, Arsenal disco, Arsenal disco' from visiting Tottenham fans. As with any variety show, the non-football entertainment on offer at Spurs down the years has been patchy in quality but, like the club itself, rarely dull:

Warren Mitchell's one-man show: Mitchell played bigoted Hammer Alf Garnett in TV hit *'til Death us Do Part* but has always been a true Spur in real life. His half-time appearances in the early 1980s to pick the winning ticket from the club's lottery draw often turned into a master class in playing to the crowd.

Break Machine: Quite why this American studio-manufactured band created in the midst of the early breakdancing boom were performing and dancing to their songs on the White Hart Lane pitch was anybody's guess, but their renditions of *Streetdance* and *Breakdance Party* in 1984 will always be remembered fondly – well by some, anyway . . .

Hit the Bar: The stuff of genius. Organised in conjunction with then shirt sponsor Holsten for the early 2000s, Hit the Bar was hosted by Martin Chivers, and involved a fan from Spurs and a supporter of the visitors attempting to chip a ball onto the crossbar from the edge of the box. Only a handful succeeded and some of the attempts had to be seen to be believed. Hit the Bar proved once and for all that fans really can't do better than the players.

— DICE WORK IF YOU CAN GET IT —

In 1990, the ever-resourceful former Spurs player and manager Terry Venables launched a board game called *The Manager*. A cross between *Trivial Pursuit* and *Monopoly* with a football-theme, the game was advertised relentlessly in the club programme.

'Terry Venables devised the game himself to recreate the action and excitement of his demanding job' said the ad. And, in a sign of the increasingly commercial times, the object was not to win trophies but to become 'the one with the most money at the end.'

— 'BORING, BORING ARSENAL' —

An inside forward for Spurs, Herbert Chapman never actually played for the other lot down the road but is arguably the most important individual in Arsenal's history (Henry Norris aside), and did much to establish their dour reputation.

Chapman joined Tottenham in March 1905 and was the team's leading goalscorer in the following Southern League season with 11 goals. Despite his distinctive yellow boots he was something of a journeyman player and after two years at Spurs and spells as manager with Northampton, Leeds and Huddersfield Town, found his spiritual home at Highbury in 1925.

It was at Arsenal that he devised his defensive 'WM' formation, sacrificing attacking ambition by fielding an extra defender to exploit the new offside law. This had reduced the number of opponents a player required between himself and the goal line from three to two and made the centre half the fulcrum of the side.

It was a philosophy that won trophies but is a direct ancestor of the long ball game and set the template for 'safety-first' football that hindered the development of the English game for a generation, until Arthur's Rowe's 'Push and run' Spurs side after the war.

— TRANSFER MILESTONES —

Tottenham's reputation as a big-spending club took a while to grow, as in the early days of the club's history many transfer fees were undisclosed. The first fee to be quoted was the £1,700 paid to Northampton Town for outside-right Fanny Walden in April 1913. Here are some other milestone cash splashes;

Date	Player	Fee	Selling club
May 1949	Alf Ramsey	£21,000	Southampton
Dec 1961	Jimmy Greaves	£99,999	AC Milan
Jan 1968	Martin Chivers	£125,000	Southampton
Mar 1970	Martin Peters	£200,000	West Ham
Sept 1976	Peter Taylor	£400,000	Crystal Palace
May 1980	Steve Archibald	£800,000	Aberdeen
Jun 1988	Paul Stewart	£1.7m	Man City
Jul 1988	Paul Gascoigne	£2m	Newcastle
Aug 1992	Teddy Sheringham	£2.1m	Notts Forest
Aug 1994	Ilie Dumitrescu	£2.6m	Steaua Bucharest
Sept 1994	Gheorge Popescu	£2.9m	PSV Eindhoven
Jun 1995	Chris Armstrong	£4.5m	Crystal Palace
Aug 1997	Les Ferdinand	£6m	Newcastle
May 2000	Sergei Rebrov	£11m	Dynamo Kiev

— LOOKING UP —

The successive fifth-place finishes in the 2005/06 and 2006/07 seasons are Tottenham's best ever in the Premiership, and the club's best top flight performance since the 1989/90 season's third place. The 2005/06 season was only the fifth in Tottenham's league history in which the team failed to score more than three goals in any game (the others being 1922/23, 1976/77, 1978/79 and 1987/88), the biggest wins coming at home against Charlton and Portsmouth – both 3–1.

Goals flowed more freely in 2006/07, Spurs scoring 3 four times, 4 twice and 5 once – this in the season's biggest win, 5–1 v Charlton. The club's lowest-ever maximum winning margin in a League season came in 1979/80, when a 4–3 victory over Coventry at White Hart Lane was as good as it got. Spurs finished that season in 14th place.

— SPURS V THE WORLD —

Tottenham have clashed with football authority on a number of occasions. Reading this list is best accompanied by the soundtrack of The Clash's *I Fought The Law (and The Law won)*.

1893: Payne's boots
Spurs are found guilty of inducing a player and professional practice (See *The Payne's Boots Affair,* page 53). The ground is closed for two weeks and Ernie Payne suspended for a week. The club's appeal is rejected.

1913: Invasion from Woolwich
The club fails in its formal objections to Woolwich Arsenal relocating to north London (See *The Seeds of A Great Rivalry*, page 5).

1919: Daylight robbery
In a break with established practice, Arsenal, who finished fifth in Division Two before the First World War, are given Tottenham's place in the top flight when the League re-starts – despite Tottenham finishing fourth from bottom of Division One. (See *The Seeds of A Great Rivalry,* page 5).

1984: No reservations
The League tick Spurs off for fielding a reserve side against Southampton for a game just days before the first leg of the UEFA Cup Final. The Saints win 5–0.

1987: The 10k break

Just before the FA Cup final, David Pleat rests a number of first team regulars for the final league game of the season against Everton. Spurs had played 17 games in the final nine weeks of the season, and all the League issues were settled. Spurs lose 1–0 and are fined £10,000.

1994: Bad law

Spurs are fined £600,000, have 12 points deducted and are banned from the FA Cup following an investigation into irregular payments to players – the most severe punishment ever handed out to any club. The punishment is later reduced to a six-point deduction, then after a second appeal, all the points are given back, and the club are re-entered into the FA Cup. The arbitration tribunal says the FA's charges were "misconceived, bad in law and should not have been proceeded with."

2005: The goal that never was

Spurs 'score' against Manchester United at Old Trafford thanks to a superb 40-yard lob from Pedro Mendes in the final minutes to record a famous victory. But United keeper Roy Carroll scoops the ball back into play and the game continues, despite the ball having clearly been over the line.

2006: It makes you sick

Spurs are forced to play their most vital game in the last 15 years with only three fit players after a virus hits the squad. They lose to West Ham and miss out on the Champions League. The decision would, of course, have been the same if Arsenal, Chelsea, Manchester United or Liverpool had been similarly affected.

— 10 DRAMATIC SPURS FANS —

Anthony Andrews
Kenneth Branagh
Bernard Bresslaw (RIP)
Pierce Brosnan
Colin Buchanan
Lenny James
Jerome Flynn
Jude Law
Sean Maguire
Leslie Phillips

— VOICE OF THE TERRACES —

The first Tottenham Hotspur fanzine, *The Spur*, appeared in May 1988, prompted not only by the surge in fan publishing but also by the club's unpopular decision to remove the Shelf, where Tottenham's most vocal support had congregated for years, and replace it with executive boxes. It lasted for another 52 issues over six years. When it ceased publication it had gone from a basic A5 black and white effort to a slick magazine with its own range of merchandise.

In January 1990, *My Eyes Have Seen The Glory* launched, publishing 28 issues until 1994. In 1998, it staged a comeback, but ceased print publication in 2007. In August 1990, *Off the Shelf* first hit the streets, publishing 12 issues until August 1992. And in August 1994, *Cock-a- Doodle-Doo* was hatched, publishing 52 issues up until the summer of 2006.

Other fanzines that have appeared over the years include:

One Flew Over Seaman's Head
Spur of the Moment
The Circumcised Cockerel
The Spurtator
F.O.G
The Cockerel Crows
News of the Screws

. . . and *Ooh, Gary Gary*, the brainchild of Barbara Ellen, then of the *NME*, now an *Observer* columnist.

— THE TOTTENHAM MEDIA MAFIA —

Eleven media wallahs who follow Spurs:

Brian Alexander (*Radio 5 Live*)
Peter Allen (*Radio 5 Live*)
Mihir Bose (*Daily Telegraph*)
Jo Whiley (*Radio 1*)
Marcus Buckland (*Sky TV*)
Derek Jameson (*Radio 2*)
Danny Kelly (*BBC Radio London*)
Michael Fish (*BBC weatherman*)
Mark Damazer, (*Radio 4 controller*)
Claire Tomlinson (*Sky TV*)
Simon Mayo (*Radio 5 Live*)

— THERE IS SOME CORNER OF A FOREIGN FIELD . . . —

. . . that is forever Tottenham. Spurs have fans all over the globe, reflecting the club's status as one of the world's most famous clubs. As Glenn Martinsen, chairman of the Norwegian branch of the supporters' club says, "I support Spurs because of their brave history and attractive way of playing the game."

Here is a selection of far-flung official supporters associations.

SWEDEN
'Tottenham Hotspur Supporters Sweden': 472 members, with at least another 2,000 fans following the club's fortunes.

NORWAY
'Tottenham's Venner' ('Friends of Tottenham'): over 2,000 members, a colour magazine, *Tottenham Supporteren*, and a website – www.tottenhamsvenner.no.

NEW YORK CITY
The NYC branch has around 50 members, with thousands of other US-based fans scattered around the country.

MALTA
Malta Spurs: 800 registered members and around another 1,500 Spurs followers.

AUSTRALIA
Oz Spurs: 250 members, an estimated 10,000 fans. More information can be found at www.ozspurs.com

HUNGARY SPURS
An official Hungarian branch is being formed, with a current estimate of 50 members.

SINGAPORE
Singapore Spurs: 130 members, estimated 500 fans. More information at www.spurs-sg.org/

— SLEEPLESS OVER SPURS —

In 1991, Kevin Keegan was infamously attacked while sleeping in his Range Rover at Reigate Hill in Surrey. He'd stopped to get some shuteye after driving 1,600 miles from Spain, and had intended to get his head down on the ferry. "My intention was to sleep on the crossing," he says, "but then I got talking to this Spurs fan. He kept asking me what I think about Tottenham and we ended up talking all the way across."

— THE PRODIGALS RETURN —

A selection of players and managers who missed life at Spurs so much, they came back for seconds

Pat Jennings
Jürgen Klinsmann
Teddy Sheringham
Neil Ruddock
Mickey Hazard
Jamie Redknapp
David Pleat
Peter McWilliam
Terry Venables
Glenn Hoddle
Steve Perryman
Chris Hughton
Arthur Rowe
Peter Shreeves

Sid McClellan
David Dunmore
John Smith
Derek Possee
Ralph Coates
Keith Osgood
John Chiedozie
Peter Taylor
Chris Jones
Pat Corbett
Tim O'Shea
Steve Hodge
Mark Stimson
Peter Garland
Ian Hendon
Scott Houghton
Jeff Minton
Jamie Clapham
Neale Fenn
Lee Barnard

— SOL, TEDDY AND CHARDONNAY —

Until it was pulled by ITV bosses in May 2006, *Footballers' Wives* thrilled TV audiences with its tales of the murky goings on at Earls Park Football Club. A feature of the show was the regular cameo appearances by celebrities such as Peter Stringfellow, Tara Palmer-Tomkinson and a host of real-life footballers including Spurs striker Teddy Sheringham and ex-Tottenham defender Sol Campbell.

Campbell put his acting skills to the test in Episode 11, 'Go for the Overkill', which was first screened on January 22nd 2003, while Teddy got to mix with glamorous duo Chardonnay and Tanya five weeks later in Episode 16, 'Fall from Grace'. Both players performed their lines reasonably competently but, perhaps unsurprisingly, neither was nominated for a BAFTA.

— CHIVVERED UP —

Secrecy surrounded the signing of striker Martin Chivers, who had made his name as one of the most dangerous strikers in the game with Southampton, as Bill Nicholson attempted to stay one step ahead of the competition.

On January 9th 1968, Chivers and Nicholson met surreptitiously at London's Waterloo station. Chivers had already informed Saints' manager Ted Bates he wanted a move, so after some initial discussions Nicholson told the big man to meet him at Bates's house the following day. From there, the two men were spirited to a Winchester hotel to formalise the deal, details having been drawn up by Nicholson and Bates when they shared a plane journey home from a scouting trip in Scotland some days before.

Meanwhile Martin's wife Carol was besieged at the couple's home by news crews who had got a sniff of a story. Much as she protested she didn't know where her husband was – it was true – the newsmen would not believe her.

Chivers signed for a British record fee of £125,000, scored on his debut at Hillsborough against Sheffield Wednesday, and went on to score 174 goals in 355 games for Spurs. He was transferred to Servette of Switzerland in 1976, and later had short spells with Norwich and Brighton. He now works as a match day host for the club, and has again achieved cult status for introducing the half-time 'Hit the bar' and 'Shoot for a Holiday' competitions.

— IN HOD WE TRUST —

The solo run against Oxford in 1986? Maybe the acrobatic volleys against Nottingham Forest and Man United in 1979 and 1980 respectively? There are plenty to choose from when it comes to selecting Glenn Hoddle's finest strike in a Spurs shirt, but one date will be forever burned in the memory of anyone who saw Hoddle play and holds the finer virtues of football close to their heart: September 24th 1983.

On that date Spurs beat Watford 3–2 at Vicarage Road, but the match, the season, even the sport itself was rendered a thing of beauty by Hoddle's goal. Feinting away from his marker on receiving the ball wide on the right, he flicked with his instep, pivoted, and from 20 yards out caressed a delicate, perfectly measured chip over Hornets keeper Steve Sherwood and into the net. Pure, unadulterated genius.

— GREAVSIE SEES RED IN BELGRADE —

The first time Jimmy Greaves was ever sent off was in Belgrade on the evening of April 25th 1963, as Spurs pursued their European Cup Winners' Cup campaign. It was a tumultuous night at the Red Army Stadium as Spurs and OFK slugged it out in the first leg of the competition's semi-final, and the sending off of Greaves capped a series of controversial decisions.

On 26 minutes, Bobby Smith was bundled over and, as Spurs prepared to take the free kick a Belgrade player fell to the floor, writhing in agony. Immediately Smith was surrounded by a swarm of angry Belgrade players who pushed and jostled him before the referee intervened. One home player tugged wildly on the ref's arm, demanding that Smith be sent off. But the referee refused, Tony Marchi took the kick, and John White volleyed the tap-in home.

OFK drew level, thanks to a penalty, before the half ended, and then in the second half came Spurs' first red card for 40 years. Referee Lajo Aranjosi later said it was for ungentlemanly conduct, claiming Greaves had kicked out at the Belgrade centre-half Krivokuca. No one else saw this, and Greaves was bemused. At first, he refused to leave the pitch, concealing himself in a crowd of Spurs players. But the referee spoke to Spurs captain Tony Marchi and finally Greaves walked from the pitch, accompanied by jeers from the 60,000 crowd.

For the remaining 35 minutes, the ten men of Spurs dominated and outclassed their opponents. Terry Dyson won them the tie, and in the return leg an inspired performance by Danny Blanchflower saw Tottenham to a 3–1 victory, and a place in the final.

— US AND THEM —

At the end of the 1951/52 season, Spurs finished second to Manchester United in Division One, trailing the league champions by only four points. In the close season, both clubs toured North America and Canada, playing each other twice. On June 14th in Toronto, Spurs won 5–0, thanks to goals from Walters, Bennett, Duquemin, Baily and Medley. The next day they played the Reds again, this time in New York, and won 7–1, with McClellan, Bennett (2) and Duquemin (4) grabbing the goals.

Watching American fans must have wondered who were the champs and who were the chumps!

— TOP FIVE SPURS READS —

1. *The Glory Game*; Hunter Davies, 1972 (Mainstream Publishing)
The original football classic, Davies's book was a revelation when published. Not only was it the first time anyone had gained such complete access to a football club's activities, it was a proper grown-up book about football.

2. *Danny Blanchflower, A Biography of a Visionary*; Dave Bowler, 1997 (Orion)
Although Danny played for other teams, he is indelibly written into the story of the first modern Double. A lovingly crafted and thoughtful account of a fine sportsman and a great man.

3. *The Glory Glory Nights*, 1986 (Cockerel Books)
The complete history of Spurs in Europe, featuring original newspaper clippings and updates from the men who played. Probably Irving Scholar's finest contribution to the club, the book was commissioned by him.

4. *Dream On, A Year in the Life of a Premier League Club*; Alex Fynn and H Davidson, 1996 (Simon & Schuster)
One of the first of the modern season diary approaches, this benefits from the twin analysis and access points of marketing man Fynn and fanzine maestro Davidson. A thoughtful and insightful account into an eventful season.

5. *Tottenham Hotspur: The Official Illustrated History 1882–1996*, Phil Soar (Hamlyn)
The updated edition of the classic *And The Spurs Go Marching On*, Soar's masterful history isn't just packed with detail and nuggets of information but is a handsome celebration of all things Spurs. It also features some outstanding photographs, particularly from the early years.

— CHIVERS TO THE RESCUE —

On April 28th 1975, as Bill Nicholson's last great side slid into decline under the management of Terry Neill, Spurs faced one of their toughest ever tasks. Anything less than a win from the game scheduled for that night would mean relegation but the opposition was Don Revie's Leeds United, who had just qualified for the European Cup final. Survival required guts as well as guile, and everyone had to play their part – including Martin Chivers, recalled for his experience despite not starting a first-team game for two months.

The team rose to the occasion, bombarding the Leeds goal after a Cyril Knowles free kick gave them a flying start after five minutes. Chivers got the second five minutes into the second half, Knowles made it 3–1 and then Chivers supplied Alfie Conn for the goal that made Spurs safe.

The team had put in a gutsy but still stylish display, and the 50,000 crowd poured onto the pitch at the final whistle, celebrating Tottenham's survival for a full half an hour before they began to disperse.

— PRAGUE SPRING —

As Spurs blazed a trail through Europe in the early 1960s, so Spurs fan Aubrey Morris helped take supporters into a new era, organising the first air charters for English football fans to follow their team in Europe.

Morris, who had fought Oswald Mosley's fascist Blackshirts on Cable Street in the famous street battle in London's East End in October 1936, been evacuated from Dunkirk, driven a cab and stood as a Communist Party candidate, was not a man to back down in the face of adversity, a quality that was to be very useful.

"In one of the games we went to Czechoslovakia," he recalls. "We were playing Dukla Prague who were the Czech champions, and when you went to Eastern Europe in those days you had to buy currency when you got there and you weren't allowed to take it away with you. They promised me they'd have somebody at the airport on the way back to change the money we hadn't spent.

"They didn't, and the pilot wouldn't wait, he said it'd cost £100 an hour to wait. Well, we just couldn't afford that, it would have been the end of us.' So Morris collected all the Czech currency from his travelling party, worked out what they were owed, and set off to sort it out himself. 'I went to the Czech embassy and harangued them and eventually we got the money back," he says.

— MISCELLANEOUS FACTS AND FIGURES —

League title winners: 2 (1950/51 & 1960/61)
Runners up: 4 (1921/22, 1951/52, 1956/57, 1962/63)
Record points: 70 (2 points for a win – 1919/20); 77 (3 points for a win – 1984/85)
Best goal difference: +70 (1919/20)
Most goals scored in a season: 115 (1960/61)
Fewest goals conceded: 32 (1908/09 & 1919/20)
Most wins: 32 (1919/20)
Fewest defeats: 4 (1919/20)
Most home wins: 19 (1919/20)
Most away wins: 16 (1960/61)
Fewest points: 28 (1914/15)
Most defeats: 22 (1934/35)
Fewest wins: 8 (1914/15)
Least goals scored: 38 (1987/88)
Most goals conceded: 95 (1958/59)

— INDIVIDUAL BRIGHT YOUNG THINGS —

In the last 34 seasons of the Football Writers' Footballer of the Year awards, only nine awards have gone to players who did not play for the Champions. And of those nine, six have played for Tottenham Hotspur. The full list is Pat Jennings (1973); Steve Perryman (1982); Clive Allen (1987); Gary Lineker (1992); Jurgen Klinsmann (1995) and David Ginola (1999). Of the other non-title-winning winners, Fulham's Alan Mullery (1975) made his name at Spurs, and Chris Waddle (1993) was a Tottenham hero, before arriving at Sheffield Wednesday, via Marseille, to lift the award. The missing name is Frans Thijssen (1981), the Ipswich maestro who would surely not have looked out of place in a Spurs shirt. All of which is grist to the mill of those who argue that the sum of Spurs teams has traditionally not been greater than the parts.

— CHAMPIONS ALL —

Full squad details for Spurs' 1950/51 League Championship-winning side.

Player	Appearances	Goals
Baily	40	12
Brittan	8	
Bennett	25	7
Burgess	35	2
Clarke	42	
Ditchburn	42	
Duquemin	33	14
McClellan	7	3
Medley	35	11
Murphy	25	9
Nicholson	41	1
Ramsey	40	4
Scarth	1	
Tickridge	1	
Uphill	2	1
Walters	40	15
Willis	39	
Withers	4	
Wright	2	1

— CHAMPIONS ALL 2 —

Full squad details for Spurs' 1960/61 League Championship-winning side.

Player	Appearances	Goals
Brown	41	
Baker	41	1
Henry	42	
Blanchflower	42	6
Norman	41	4
Mackay	37	4
Jones	29	15
White	42	13
Smith R	36	28
Allen	42	22
Dyson	40	12
Medwin	14	5
Saul	6	3
Marchi	6	
Dodge		
Atkinson		
Collins		
Hollowbread	1	
Barton	1	
Smith J	1	

— THE LEAGUE RECORD SEASON BY SEASON —

		Home					Away							
SEASON (DIV)	P	W	D	L	F	A	W	D	L	F	A	Pts	GD	Pos.
1908/09 (2)	38	12	5	2	42	12	8	6	5	25	20	51	35	2nd
(promoted)														
1909/10 (1)	38	10	6	3	35	23	1	4	14	18	46	32	-16	15th
1910/11 (1)	38	10	5	4	40	23	3	1	15	12	40	32	-11	15th
1911/12 (1)	38	10	4	5	35	20	4	5	10	18	33	37	0	12th
1912/13 (1)	38	9	3	7	28	25	3	3	13	17	47	30	-27	17th
1913/14 (1)	38	9	6	4	30	19	3	4	12	20	43	34	-12	17th
1914/15 (1)	38	7	7	5	30	29	1	5	13	27	61	28	-33	20th
(relegated*)														
1919/20 (2)	42	19	2	0	60	11	13	4	4	42	21	70	70	1st
(promoted)														
1920/21 (1)	42	15	2	4	46	16	4	7	10	24	32	47	22	6th
1921/22 (1)	42	15	3	3	43	17	6	6	9	22	22	51	26	2nd
(runner up)														
1922–23 (1)	42	11	3	7	34	22	6	4	11	16	28	41	0	12th
1923/24 (1)	42	9	6	6	30	22	3	8	10	20	34	38	-6	15th
1924/25 (1)	42	9	8	4	32	16	6	4	11	20	27	42	9	12th
1925/26 (1)	42	11	4	6	45	36	4	5	12	21	43	39	-13	15th
1926/27 (1)	42	11	4	6	48	33	5	5	11	28	45	41	-2	13th
1927/28 (1)	42	12	3	6	47	34	3	5	13	27	52	38	-12	21st
(relegated)														
1928/29 (2)	42	16	3	2	50	26	1	6	14	25	55	43	-6	10th
1929/30 (2)	42	11	8	2	43	24	4	1	16	16	37	39	-2	12th
(lowest lge. pos.)														
1930/31 (2)	42	15	5	1	64	20	7	2	12	24	35	51	33	3rd
1931/32 (2)	42	11	6	4	58	37	5	5	11	29	41	43	9	8th
1932/33 (2)	42	14	7	0	58	19	6	8	7	38	32	55	45	2nd
(promoted)														
1933/34 (1)	42	14	3	4	51	24	7	4	10	28	32	49	23	3rd
1934/35 (1)	42	8	8	5	34	31	2	2	17	20	62	30	39	22nd
(relegated)														
1935/36 (2)	42	12	6	3	60	25	6	7	8	31	30	49	36	5th
1936/37 (2)	42	13	3	5	57	26	4	6	11	31	40	43	22	10th
1937/38 (2)	42	14	3	4	46	16	5	3	13	30	38	44	22	5th
1938/39 (2)	42	13	6	2	48	27	6	3	12	19	35	47	5	8th
1939/40 (2)	3	0	1	0	1	1	1	1	0	5	4	4	1	7th
(season abandoned)														

1946/47	(2)	42	11	8	2	35	21	6	6	9	30	32	48	12	6th
1947/48	(2)	42	10	6	5	36	24	5	8	8	20	19	44	13	8th
1948/49	(2)	42	14	4	3	50	18	3	12	6	22	26	50	28	5th
1949/50	(2)	42	15	3	3	51	15	12	4	5	30	20	61	46	1st
(promoted)															
1950/51	(1)	42	17	2	2	54	21	8	8	5	28	23	60	38	1st
(Champions)															
1951/52	(1)	42	16	1	4	45	20	6	8	7	31	31	53	25	2nd
(runner up)															
1952/53	(1)	42	11	6	4	55	37	4	5	12	23	32	41	9	10th
1953/54	(1)	42	11	3	7	38	33	5	2	14	27	43	37	-11	16th
1954/55	(1)	42	9	4	8	42	35	7	4	10	30	38	40	-1	16th
1955/56	(1)	42	9	4	8	37	33	6	3	12	24	38	37	-10	18th
1956/57	(1)	42	15	4	2	70	24	7	8	6	34	32	56	48	2nd
(runner up)															
1957/58	(1)	42	13	4	4	58	33	8	5	8	35	44	51	16	3rd
1958/59	(1)	42	10	3	8	56	42	3	7	11	29	53	36	-10	18th
1959/60	(1)	42	10	6	5	43	24	11	5	5	43	26	53	36	3rd
1960/61	(1)	42	15	3	3	65	28	16	1	4	50	27	66	60	1st
(Champions)															
1961/62	(1)	42	14	4	3	59	34	7	6	8	29	35	52	19	3rd
1962/63	(1)	42	14	6	1	72	28	9	3	9	39	34	55	49	2nd
(runner up)															
1963/64	(1)	42	13	3	5	54	31	9	4	8	43	50	51	16	4th
1964/65	(1)	42	18	3	0	65	20	1	4	16	22	51	45	16	6th
1965/66	(1)	42	11	6	4	55	37	5	6	10	20	29	44	9	8th
1966/67	(1)	42	15	3	3	44	21	9	5	7	27	27	56	23	3rd
1967/68	(1)	42	11	7	3	44	20	8	2	11	26	39	47	11	7th
1968/69	(1)	42	10	8	3	39	22	4	9	8	22	29	45	10	6th
1969/70	(1)	42	11	2	8	27	21	6	7	8	27	34	43	-1	11th
1970/71	(1)	42	11	5	5	33	19	8	9	4	21	14	52	21	3rd
1971/72	(1)	42	16	3	2	45	13	3	10	8	18	29	51	21	6th
1972/73	(1)	42	10	5	6	33	23	6	8	7	25	25	45	10	8th
1973/74	(1)	42	9	4	8	26	27	5	10	6	19	23	42	-5	11th
1974/75	(1)	42	8	4	9	29	27	5	4	12	23	36	34	-11	19th
1975/76	(1)	42	6	10	5	33	32	8	5	8	30	31	43	0	9th
1976/77	(1)	42	9	7	5	26	20	3	2	16	22	52	33	-24	22nd
(relegated)															
1977/78	(2)	42	13	7	1	50	19	7	9	5	33	30	56	34	3rd
(promoted)															
1978/79	(1)	42	7	8	6	19	25	6	7	8	29	36	41	-13	11th
1979/80	(1)	42	11	5	5	30	22	4	5	12	22	40	40	-10	14th

1980/81	(1)	42	9	9	3	44	31	5	6	10	26	37	43	2	10th
1981/82	(1)	42	12	4	5	41	26	8	7	6	26	22	71	19	4th
1982/83	(1)	42	15	4	2	50	15	5	5	11	15	35	69	15	4th
1983/84	(1)	42	11	4	6	31	24	6	6	9	33	41	61	-1	8th
1984/85	(1)	42	11	3	7	46	31	12	5	4	32	20	77	27	3rd
1985/86	(1)	42	12	2	7	47	25	7	6	8	27	27	65	22	10th
1986/87	(1)	42	14	3	4	40	14	7	5	9	28	29	71	25	3rd
1987/88	(1)	40	9	5	6	26	23	3	6	11	12	25	47	-10	13th
1988/89	(1)	38	8	6	5	31	24	7	6	6	29	22	57	14	6th
1989/90	(1)	38	12	1	6	35	24	7	5	7	24	23	63	13	3rd
1990/91	(1)	38	8	9	2	35	22	3	7	9	16	28	49	1	10th
1991/92	(1)	42	7	3	11	33	35	8	4	9	25	28	52	-5	15th
1992/93	(1)	42	11	5	5	40	25	5	6	10	20	41	59	-6	8th
1993/94	(1)	42	4	8	9	29	33	7	4	10	25	26	45	-5	15th
1994/95	(1)	42	10	5	6	32	25	6	9	6	34	33	62	8	7th
1995/96	(1)	38	9	5	5	26	19	7	8	4	24	19	61	12	8th
1996/97	(1)	38	8	4	7	19	17	5	3	11	25	34	46	-7	10th
1997/98	(1)	38	7	8	4	23	22	4	3	12	21	34	44	-9	14th
1998/99	(1)	38	7	7	5	28	26	4	7	8	19	24	47	-3	11th
1999/00	(1)	38	10	3	6	40	26	5	5	9	17	23	53	8	10th
2000/01	(1)	38	11	6	2	31	16	2	4	13	16	38	49	-7	12th
2001/02	(1)	38	10	4	5	32	24	4	4	11	17	29	50	-4	9th
2002/03	(1)	38	9	4	6	30	29	5	4	10	21	33	50	-11	10th
2003/04	(1)	38	9	4	6	33	27	4	2	13	14	30	45	-10	14th
2004/05	(1)	38	9	5	5	36	22	5	5	9	11	19	52	6	9th
2005/06	(1)	38	12	5	2	31	16	6	6	7	22	22	65	15	5th
2006/07	(1)	38	12	3	4	34	22	5	6	8	23	32	60	3	5th

*Spurs relegated despite expansion of the league (See *The Seeds of A Great Rivalry*, page 2)

Selected Bibliography

A Century of Great Soccer Drama, John Cottrell, Rupert Hart-Davis Ltd, 1970

Danny Blanchflower, A biography of a Visionary, Dave Bowler, Orion, 1997

Dream On, Alex Fynn & H. Davidson, Simon & Schuster, 1996

The England Compendium, Clive Batty, VSP,. 2006

The Essential History of Tottenham Hotspur, Bob Goodwin, Headline 2001

The Football Grounds of England and Wales, Simon Inglis, Collins Willow, 1985; 1996

The Glory Game, Hunter Davies, Mainstream 2000

The Glory, Glory Nights, Cockerel Books, 1986

The Real Mackay, Dave Mackay and Martin King, Mainstream, 2004

Spurs, A Complete Record, Bob Goodwin, Breedon Books, 1988

The Tottenham Hotspur Football Book No 5, Stanley Paul, 1971

Tottenham Hotspur, The Official Illustrated History 1882–1997, Phil Soar, Hamlyn

The Official Tottenham Hotspur Fans Guide, Gerry Cox, Carlton, 1997

Tottenham Hotspur Official Annual, 1982, Circle Publications

Tottenham Hotspur Official Annual, '83, Circle Publications

The Book of Football Quotations, Phil Shaw, Ebury Press, 2003

Rothmans Football Yearbook (various editions), Editors: Jack & Glenda Rollin, Headline

Tottenham Hotspur Football Club 1882–1952, Roy Brazil, Tempus, 2005

Tottenham Hotspur Head-to-Head, Peter Waring, Breedon Books, 2004

Spurs The 25 Year Record, Editor Michael Robinson, 1997

Match of The Day, John Motson, BBC Books, 1992

The History of the Latymer School at Edmonton, JA Morris, 1975

OTHER SOURCES

www.topspurs.com

www.mehstg.co.uk

www.spursodyssey.co.uk